WORLD CUP
France1998

MARK TROWBRIDGE

SELECT
EDITIONS

This edition published 1998 by
PRC Publishing Ltd,
Kiln House, 210 New Kings Road, London SW6 4NZ
exclusively for Selecta Book Ltd, Folly Road, Roundway,
Devizes, Wiltshire SN10 2HR

ISBN 1 85648 468 8

Printed and bound in Spain

CONTENTS

HISTORY

The birth of the World Cup in its modern form took place in Uruguay on 13 July 1930. The opening tie involved France (as a mark of honour to Bastille day on the 14th), whose opponents on this historical occasion were Mexico. It fell to Frenchman Laurent to become the first ever goal scorer in a World Cup finals tournament. The formation of the debut competition had been purely on an invitation basis and many of Europe's leading countries declined to participate. It was left to a paltry 13 countries to contest the competition. The seeded nations came from the Americas (Argentina, Brazil, USA and hosts Uruguay). All reached the semi-final stages except the fancied Brazilians, who were eliminated by the Yugoslavians (one of only four European nations to appear, the others being Belgium, Romania and France). The first ever World Cup Final, played in Montevideo, saw Argentina play against Uruguay. A crowd of approximately 100,000 saw the Olympic soccer champions of 1928 — Uruguay — claim victory. Uruguay skipper Nasazzi became the first captain to hold aloft the Jules Rimet trophy. It would prove to be a further 20 years before another Uruguayan hand would receive the coveted prize.

British teams did not participate in 1930, and again declined the offer of participation in the next competition staged in Italy four years later. Nevertheless, the second finals were far more representative with nations from South America, North America, Europe and Africa taking part. The key absentees were holders Uruguay, who refused to attend: 'Europe snubbed our tournament so we shall do the same' was the offered excuse. The shape of the proceedings had also been altered; where before there were group stages, the 1934 tournament had a straightforward knock out system. Italy spluttered through the second round, and semi-finals to reach the final in Rome. New features of the Italian side were several Argentines (claiming dual nationality) who had starred for them in the final four years earlier. These adopted talents helped guide Italy to the crown in front of the 55,000-strong crowd.

With the threat of war looming over the 1938 tournament in France, the competition was without a number of national sides. Spain through civil war, Austria due to Nazi occupation and England again declined the offer — still in dispute with FIFA. South America's lone entry was Brazil (Uruguay still chose to boycott the European-based competitions). Holders Italy proved to be a more attractive proposition than four years earlier, and reached their second successive World Cup Final, this time against Hungary. The final was to staged at the newly built Colombes stadium in Paris, and attracted a crowd of 45,000. After a hard battle, the Italians finally took control and recorded a 4-2 victory. The side based on strength and speed had set the standard for future Italian sides to follow.

ABOVE: Brazil is the most successful side in World Cup history with four wins. Here Romario celebrates their 1994 triumph over Italy.

It would be 12 years before the World Cup was next held: the war and its aftermath saw the competition suspended until 1950. When it resumed, the tournament returned to South America, 20 years after the inaugural event, this time with Brazil as hosts. The 1950 tournament reinstated the group format — so that even unsuccessful teams could look forward to more than a single knock-out game after weeks of travel to get to the tournament. For the first time, the British Isles were represented: England aimed to impose its reputation on a world stage, but many other nations were missing including Austria, Russia and, of course, divided Germany. The Italian side had been wrecked by the Supergra air crash in which the main heart of the squad had been destroyed (the formidable Torino side lost 17 members in the tragedy).

Brazil and England started the tournament as favourites, but nobody could have predicted stunning future events. England, who had conquered Chile in their first ever World Cup match, faced the minnows of the USA. England failed to cope with the climate and conditions, and were defeated. To progress further they had to beat Spain: England went down to a solitary goal and faced that long journey home.

Brazil's form had been far more impressive but, in front of a staggering 200,000 fans at the Maracana, Uruguay spoiled the party by claiming two second half goals to snatch the Jules Rimet trophy.

The World Cup returned to Europe for the 1954 tournament, based in Switzerland. It proved a goal scoring success with the team of the moment being Hungary, with such famous names as Puskas, Hideguti, Czibor and Koscis. The 'Magical Magyars' eased their way to the final, where they faced a West German side that they had already thrashed 8-3 in the group stages. With Puskas suffering from medical problems, Hungary wilted and lost out to the tenacity and endeavour typical of German sides. Fritz Walter became the first of three German captains to hold aloft the top prize in world football.

The 1958 tournament will surely be remembered for two things: the emergence of the Brazilian style of footballing magic, and the diminutive figure of a certain Edson Arantes do Nascimento — better known as Pele. At just 17 the youngster was about to set the world alight with his unique brilliance. A significant feature for the British Isles was the participation of all four home nations although only Wales and Northern Ireland progressed beyond round two.

The Irish had their progression ended by the French side which paraded the talents of Raymond Kopa and the competition's top scorer Just Fontaine (a tally of 13 which is still to be bettered). The awesome French were finally dispatched by the breathtaking Brazilians at the semi-final stage. New hero Pele proved the difference with a hat-trick. Hosts Sweden were slowly growing in confidence, avoiding the Brazilians until they met in the final in Stockholm, where the Swedes took a surprise lead before finally buckling under the pressure. Brazil's style was rewarded with five goals — two by Pele. At the final whistle he wept tears of joy, an image long to be remembered in World Cup history.

With the competition returning to South America (Chile), Brazil could sense the perfect opportunity to be the first nation to retain the Jules Rimet trophy. They reached the final easily: their opponents were the wily Czechs who had accounted for the fancied Yugoslavs and Hungarians. The final in Santiago was to be one match too many for the Czechs; despite taking the lead, they lost to three Brazilian goals.

The World Cup of 1966 started sensationally when the Jules Rimet trophy was stolen while on exhibition in London; thankfully a dog named 'Pickles' discovered the trophy hidden under a bush. England coach Alf Ramsey had gone on record to say that he believed his England side could lift the World Cup. So it proved: England kept out every opponent, until Eusebio scored from the penalty spot in the semi-finals. They were met in the final by the efficient West Germans whose side contained Seeler, Overath, Schnellinger and, of course, Beckenbauer. The rest is history. The Germans took the lead through Haller; England promptly equalised through Hurst, and looked to have grabbed victory with Peters' strike, but with seconds to spare Weber sent the game into extra-time. What followed was one of the most controversial moments in World Cup history. Hurst's swivel and shot from Ball's pass, flew past goalkeeper Tilkowski and crashed down from the crossbar. Did it cross the line? The whole of England held its breath as the officials conferred —

**ABOVE: German sides have won three world cups —
here Beckenbauer and the 1974 team line up after
beating Holland 2-1.**

and the goal was given. Hurst went on to rifle home
England's fourth to become the first and only person
so far to achieve a hat-trick in a World Cup Final.

The Brazil side in the 1970 Mexico tournament,
exhibited some of the most breathtaking and
enchanting football ever seen. Under the guidance
of the rejuvenated Pele, they tore into every opponent with gusto reaching the final almost as a formality: but who would they meet? The ever competitive West Germans came back from two goals down
to destroy England's hopes of retaining the trophy
and met Italy in the semi-final. With Beckenbauer
nursing an injured shoulder, West Germany finally
succumbed to a winner by Rivera.

The final, in the Azteca stadium in Mexico City,
provided one of the most clinical displays in a World
Cup football. Brazil's fluid passing, composure and
control had the Italians chasing shadows. This was
Brazil's third triumph in the World Cup Final, and as
a mark of honour were allowed to keep the Jules
Rimet Trophy.

Expectations were high for 1974 to produce the
same level of play displayed four years earlier.
Brazil's team had changed with Rivelino and
Jairzinho (who scored in every round in 1970 — the
only player to do so) the two main existing compo-
nents of the squad. They were joined by the 'total
football' of the Dutch and the powerful home nation
— West Germany. Brazil did not prove as strong as
in 1970, and were eliminated in the second set of
pool matches, finally finishing fourth behind West
Germany, Holland and Poland. The new champions
would come from either the Dutch or the hosts, as
the two met head on in the Olympic Stadium in
Munich. The match was won by the devilish Gerd
Muller, whose sharp turn and shot left goalkeeper
Jongbloed stranded. His leaps of delight brought joy
to veteran coach Helmut Schoen, and saw the
Germans claim the new World Cup trophy.

The tournament of 1978 was hosted by
Argentina. Holland once again were the team to
watch, and they reached the final at the River Plate,
an occasion remembered for its ticker-tape welcome

of the Argentine side. The final was a tense affair with both teams creating chances: Kempes struck first for Argentina, Nanninga levelled for Holland. With seconds remaining of normal time Rensenbrink struck a post for the Dutch, and their momentum was gone. Mario Kempes split the Holland defence to net his second, and Bertoni clinched the victory with a third in the dying moments. Coach Cesar Luis Menotti had directed his team to a victory under immense pressure from government officials; despite the political affairs football proved the winner.

Argentina was looking to hold on to its trophy in Spain in 1982, now with the dazzling Diego Maradona in their squad. Although the cunning Argentine showed early promise he was sent off, and Argentina had let their crown slip. It was time for new heroes to emerge, and Italy found one in goal scorer Paolo Rossi; he returned to fire six goals, including a hat-trick over the rejuvenated Brazilians (Zico et al). The UK was represented by Scotland, England (whose Bryan Robson score the fastest goal in World Cup history) and Northern Ireland, who produced a shock defeat of hosts Spain. England found themselves eliminated without losing a game.

Spain '82 saw the appearance of the breathtaking France side inspired by the intricate midfield of Platini, Six and Giresse. They were finally beaten by West Germany in the semi-finals — this was to be the first tie decided on penalty kicks (Hrubesch scored the decisive goal). The final matched Italy with West Germany in Madrid. Flowing football balanced with discipline saw the Italians triumph. Dino Zoff became the oldest captain to lift the trophy, and the third occasion a captain from Italy has done so.

Maradona put the tribulations of Spain behind him and led his Argentine side into battle in Mexico '86. Maradona sparkled and influenced those around him. There were goals a plenty during the 1986 tournament and some thrilling matches, and decisive incidents — none more so than the two faces of Maradona exposed against England. First there was the infamous 'Hand of God' incident, for which Maradona will always be remembered, when he punched the ball over England goalkeeper Peter Shilton. Secondly, there was his mesmeric dance through the English defence to score a scintillating second. Maradona continued this incredible form all the way to the final at the Azteca, where their opponents would be the indestructible West Germans. The final pitted flamboyance with honest endeavour, although in Karl Heinz Rumminigge Germany had a true footballing master. It was he who revived West Germany when two goals down. Rudi Voller headed the German's level. The last word was with Maradona whose inch-perfect pass allowed Burruchaga to snatch a late winner.

The Argentines again reached the final in 1990, but without the style of four years previously; this time it was West Germany who possessed the genuine finished article. Ruthless efficiency and powerful play combined with skill and speed, and a mastermind in the form of Franz Beckenbauer, who coached his side with style all the way to the top. There were few scares for the Germans except the

ABOVE: Dino Zoff becomes the oldest captain to hold aloft the World Cup in Spain '82.

penalty shoot-out triumph over the luckless England. The driving force was Lothar Matthaus, a positive tank of player, and the goals of Jurgen Klinsmann. The continent of Africa provided a stiff challenge — the shape of things to come — and Cameroon gained an astonishing victory over Argentina, Maradona and all. Their colour and enthusiasm set the tournament alight. Despite this setback Argentina progressed to a dull final, enlivened in the wrong way with two Argentine players red-carded. Andreas Brehme scored the West German winner from the penalty spot.

USA '94 was hyped to being the most organised, the most spectacular and most successful championship in the World Cup's history. It was left for the Brazilians to recapture the winning ways that had deserted them in recent tournaments. Adopting a more defensive approach, Brazil clinched a record fourth title, mainly inspired by the sprightly Romario and the solid captain Dunga. Shock sides Nigeria and Bulgaria both displayed their potential — Bulgaria reached the semi-finals, before losing to Italy, who ran out of luck in the first ever final decided by penalties. Their key figure Roberto Baggio missed the decisive kick to hand the trophy to Brazil.

The Brazilians will be looking again to reproduce the same winning form in France, and claim a fifth World Cup, but as always there will be plenty of teams attempting to stop them including the Dutch, hosts France, Germany, England and even a dark horse such as Romania or Yugoslavia.

FRANCE

WORLD CUP HISTORY
Previous finals: 1930, 1934, 1938, 1954, 1958, 1966,
1978, 1982, 1986
Best performance: 3rd place 1958, 1986

As all host nations will testify, the onus is definitely on them to perform well: in every tournament the host country has always proceeded to the second round, and this should not prove an issue for a French side still living in the shadowy of its dazzling counterpart of the 1980s.

The French national side has always flattered to deceive, always promising much but delivering little. Their last venture on the World Cup stage was in 1986, and the side which fielded the likes of Platini, Tigana and Rocheteau performed with style and grace before losing unluckily to the West Germans in the semifinals. Two years earlier Platini et al had set Europe alight with their artistry and claimed the European Nations' crown. Over 15 years have elapsed since then and France is still looking for that coveted return to glory. One man who could possibly enable them to recapture that unique Gallic magic is the elusively creative Youri Djorkaeff — but the current France squad lacks a Fontaine or a Papin, to utilise his efforts fully. PSG's Florien Maurice, Monaco's young starlet Thierry Henry, target man Christophe Dugarry (Barcelona) or Espanyol-based Nicolas Oudec will all be vying to fill the role which has never been adequately filled since JPP's absence from the international arena.

The man behind the French bid for glory is coach Aime Jacquet, who led them to qualification, and the semi-finals of the European

Championships in 1996 where they lost on penalties to the Czech Republic. Many observers do not see him as the figure to steer them to success, as France have proved unconvincing in the friendly matches, which are so vital for their preparations — as host nation they have not had to play qualification games and competitive matches.

LEFT: France before playing against Brazil in 1997's Le Tournoi.

BELOW: Youri Djorkaeff in a friendly against Sweden, April 1997. France won 2–0.

Despite the lack of a genuine goal scorer, France has a wealth of talent to fall back on — such as the inconsistent Zinedine Zidane, the youthful exuberance of Robert Pires and Ibrahim Ba, as well as 'Man Mountain' Marcel Desailly. If the French are to succeed in the summer of 1998, the whole of France must get behind them or it could be yet another case of so near and yet so far!

ABOVE: Marcel Desailly in action against Italy during the 2–2 draw in June 1997's Le Tournoi. Big and strong, much will be expected of Desailly in France's World Cup challenge.

LEFT: Another photograph taken during Le Tournoi: Here, Zinedine Zidane plays in France's 1–1 draw with World Cup favourites Brazil.

PLAYERS TO WATCH FOR

Youri Djorkaeff

Marcel Desailly

Zinedine Zidane

FIRST ROUND MATCHES

Date	Opponents	Venue
12.6	South Africa	Marseille
18.6	Saudi Arabia	Saint-Denis
24.6	Denmark	Lyon

BRAZIL

WORLD CUP HISTORY
Previous finals: 1930, 1934, 1938, 1950, 1954, 1958,
1962, 1966, 1970, 1974, 1978, 1982, 1986, 1990, 1994
Best performance: Winners 1958, 1962, 1970, 1994

As holders and perennial pre-tournament favourites, the onus will be firmly on Brazil to repeat the success of the World Cup winning side, and even recreating the panache and the style of the class of 1970. Often seen as everyone's 'second favourite team' the Nike-backed Brazil will have a great deal to live up to. However, the new breed of Brazilian national side has a new stability in its play — gone are the days of a more 'gung-ho' approach to the game. With the likes of Aldair and Celio Silva forming a solid central defence partnership, a more European style of play has been adopted. This was clearly illustrated in Brazil's success during the 1994 tournament: although fewer goals were scored, less were conceded. Despite this new willingness to keep clean sheets, it's in the striking department that Brazil are spoilt for choice. Always renowned for attacking potential, Brazil can call upon the world's most expensive players in Denilson (Real Betis) and Ronaldo, now at Inter Milan following his 'megabucks' move from Barcelona, coupled with the re-emergence of the elder statesman Romario (Brazil's star player during USA 1994), as well as the up and coming Adilton (a revelation for Brazil during their World Youth Cup campaign in Malaysia). The Parma striker could even eclipse his Brazilian counterparts if he's given the chance in France, with the Barcelona duo of Sonny

Anderson and Rivaldo also waiting in the wings.

Another key to Brazil's 'imminent' success are their two foraging full backs, Cafu (AS Roma) and Roberto Calos (Real Madrid). Both follow in the Brazilian tradition of attacking full backs — Jorginho and Leonardo performed the same duties in 1994 as, of course, did the dynamic Alberto Carlos (captain of the 1970 Brazilians). As well as pace, skill and technique, Brazil can also call upon Roberto Carlos's 'cannonball' shot, which has numerous opposing keepers shuddering at the prospect.

LEFT: The Brazilian team that won the World Cup in America in 1994.

BELOW: Ronaldo playing in Le Tournoi against Italy in their 3-3 draw.

If Brazil do have a weakness, it would lie in the central midfield positions. During Le Tournoi these berths were filled by the ageing Dunga, and the not so sprightly Mauro Silva; however if need be both these positions could be filled by Leonardo (generally seen as a more orthodox winger) and the young Djalmins, both relying on skill rather than endeavour.

Following Carlos Alberto Parreira's successful stint as coach in 1994, Mario Zagalo is back at the helm and will be looking to repeat the double triumph he experienced as a player in 1958 and as coach of the 'Dream Team' in 1970. The wily Zagalo has plenty of attacking options, and may well shuffle his pack to find a partner for the irrepressible Ronaldo. If Brazil does triumph, this could be the team for the 21st century.

ABOVE: Cafu playing against England in the 1-0 win at Le Tournoi in June 1997.

LEFT: Roberto Carlos playing against France in Le Tournoi in June 1997.

PLAYERS TO WATCH FOR
Ronaldo

Roberto Carlos

Cafu

Leonardo

FIRST ROUND MATCHES

Date	Opponents	Venue
10.6	Scotland	Saint-Denis
16.6	Morocco	Nantes
23.6	Norway	Marseille

GERMANY

Following their failure to retain in USA '94 the cup they had won four years earlier, the Germans will hope to re-create the form they showed during their triumphant Euro '96 campaign. Despite their success they showed only rare glimpses of the stunning play of which they are capable. However, it was Germany's ruthless efficiency and cohesion, which saw them lift the trophy for the third time. Once again their achievement was under the supervision of demanding coach Berti Vogts, who led them to the European Championships Final in 1992 (they lost 2-0 to Denmark), the World Cup quarter finals in USA '94, glory in England during the European Nations in 1996 and now to the finals in France.

Qualification for the 1998 competition was not as straightforward as it had proved in previ-

WORLD CUP HISTORY
Previous finals: 1934, 1938, 1954, 1958, 1962, 1966, 1970, 1974, 1978, 1982, 1986, 1990, 1994
Best performance: Winners 1954, 1974, 1990

EUROPE GROUP 9

TEAM	P	W	D	L	G	PTS
Germany	10	6	4	0	23-9	22
Ukraine	10	6	2	2	10-6	20
Portugal	10	5	4	1	12-4	19
Armenia	10	1	5	4	8-17	8
N Ireland	10	1	4	5	6-10	7
Albania	10	1	1	8	7-20	4

THE ROAD TO FRANCE

9.9.96	Armenia	(a)	1-5 (w)	7.6.96	Ukraine	(a)	0-0 (d)
9.11.96	N Ireland	(h)	1-1 (d)	20.8.96	N Ireland	(a)	1-3 (w)
9.12.96	Portugal	(a)	0-0 (d)	6.9.97	Portugal	(h)	1-1 (d)
2.4.96	Albania	(a)	2-3 (w)	10.9.97	Armenia	(h)	4-0 (w)
30.4.96	Ukraine	(h)	2-0 (w)	11.10.97	Albania	(h)	4-3 (w)

ous years. Germany's final tie against Albania should have been a formality, yet they struggled against one of Europe's weaker soccer nations. They had to rely upon a last minute header from Oliver Bierhoff (Germany's match winner in the Euro '96 final), to seal a 4–3 victory following a spirited comeback by the Albanians. In spite of this current lack of stability, the Germans will surely once again be one of the pre-tournament favourites. They will also be aiming to improve their already impressive World Cup record: they have three victories under their belt, have appeared in the final on three further occasions (1966, 1982 and 1986) as well as reaching the semi-finals stage three times (1934, 1958 and 1970). So Germany certainly have the World Cup pedigree to back up their efforts. The key to all their success has been their hard work, efficiency and cohesion. It would seem to many that Germany field 11 captains: each player is a leader. This coupled with a vast amount of experience within their camp, makes them a formidable team unit.

The foundation of the German team is based

ABOVE LEFT: German team that played Portugal in their group qualifier in September 1997.

BELOW: Thomas Hassler playing in the 4-0 win against Albania in September 1997.

on its impregnable defensive system. Germany combines rigid discipline, solid tackling and forceful marking to foil opponents' attacking aspirations. The team can call upon several vastly experienced defenders, such as the elegant Matthias Sammer (an integral part of the side in Euro '96), who is currently struggling with injury problems, the dominating Thomas Helmer, man marker Jurgen Kohler, the mature Stefan Reuter and the classy Christian Ziege. The young Milan star is the route of many of Germany's goalscoring chances. His storming runs cause numerous difficulties for opposing defences. Aiming to make the most of this quality supply is a band of strikers, which includes the masterly Jurgen Klinsmann. Klinsmann will be paired with either the towering Oliver Bierhoff, the surging Ulf Kirsten or younger strikers Lars Ricken (who offered a glimpse of his ability versus Juventus in the European Cup Final of 1997. The young Dortmund striker scored with a spectacular chip with his first touch, after coming on as a substitute!) and Heiko Herrlich also at Borussia Dortmund.

Given the task of providing the ammunition for Klinsmann and his fellow strikers will be the cunning Thomas Haessler — a master of dead ball situations; alongside Haessler will be workhorse Dieter Eilts, such an influence on German's Euro '96 triumph, he will provide the cover to allow Haessler freedom to exploit any weakness shown by their opponents.

Nobody will relish meeting the steely Germans whose guile and strength should see them progress to at least the semi-final stages, and maybe their fourth tournament victory.

ABOVE: Jurgen Klinsmann playing against Russia in their 2-0 win in June 1997.

LEFT: Oliver Bierhoff before playing against Portugal in September 1997.

PLAYERS TO WATCH FOR

Thomas Haessler

Christian Ziege

Jurgen Kohler

FIRST ROUND MATCHES

Date	Opponents	Venue
15.6	USA	Paris
21.6	Yugoslavia	Lens
25.6	Iran	Montpellier

SPAIN

So many times Spain have promised so much, but have failed to live up to their expectations. With a flourishing Primera Liga and their teams performing well in European club competitions, the onus is on the national side to reap international rewards. They clearly have an abundance of quality attributes to call upon. The balance of youth and experience within the Spanish squad should steer them to long overdue success.

Spain failed to distinguish themselves at Euro '96 and were knocked out in the second stage. Before then, they were dealt a poor hand in USA '94. They advanced to the second phase without impressing, then beat Switzerland. This was followed by controversy in the quarter finals versus Italy. With the score standing all square, Luis Enrique was struck in the face by defender Mauro Tassotti inside the Italian penalty area; the match officials failed to see the incident and within seconds Italy had

WORLD CUP HISTORY
Previous finals: 1934, 1950, 1962, 1966, 1978, 1982, 1986, 1990, 1994
Best performance: 4th 1950

EUROPE GROUP 6

TEAM	P	W	D	L	G	PTS
Spain	**10**	**8**	**2**	**0**	**26-6**	**26**
Yugoslavia	10	7	2	1	29-7	23
Czech Rep	10	5	1	4	16-6	16
Slovakia	10	5	1	4	18-14	16
Faroe Iss	10	2	0	8	10-31	6
Malta	10	0	0	10	2-37	0

THE ROAD TO FRANCE

4.9.96	Faroe Is	(a)	2-6 (w)	12.2.97	Malta	(h)	4-0 (w)
9.10.96	Czech Rep	(a)	0-0 (d)	30.4.97	Yugoslavia	(a)	1-1 (d)
13.11.96	Slovakia	(h)	4-1 (w)	8.6.97	Czech Rep	(h)	1-0 (w)
14.12.96	Yugoslavia	(h)	2-0 (w)	24.9.97	Slovakia	(a)	1-2 (w)
18.12.96	Malta	(a)	0-3 (w)	11.10.97	Faroe Is	(h)	3-1 (w)

gained a winning advantage. Had the referee seen the act, Spain would have been awarded a penalty, Tassotti would have been dismissed and the course of the game would have been altered. To rub salt into the wounds Tassotti was later handed an eight-match international ban!

Coach Javier Clemente has ushered Spain to the World Cup for the ninth time in their history. He has toyed with the Spanish formation, as many international managers have done, experimenting with the popular wing-back system. In Sergi Barjuan he has the ideal protagonist to fill this role; indeed, Barjuan's surging runs have even seen him appear in more central attacking areas. This quality of versatility could also be attributed to Barcelona teammate Luis Enrique, who has developed into one of Europe's finest performers. An occasional wing back, Enrique can be seen more prominently in his opponents' defensive third. Versatility is a focal point of Spain's side: a number of players can perform in a selection of roles, allowing Clemente

ABOVE LEFT: The Spanish team against Faroe Islands in the group qualifier in October 1997.

BELOW: Oliverio Alvarez playing in the 3-1 win against the Faroe Islands in October 1997.

to shuffle his pack to produce results so badly desired.

Spain's captain, the effective Fernando Hierro, is gifted with an educated footballing brain, strength, positional awareness and precise ball distribution. He can operate both in central defensive or midfield roles. To accompany Hierro, Clemente can look to a band of uncompromising defenders: Roberto Rios, Rafael Alkorta, Abelardo and the hard-nosed Miguel Nadal. All would provide watertight cover for the elegant Hierro. The 'keeper for Spain is the formidable Andoni Zubizarreta, a major influence in Spain's defence

Spain have no problems in protecting their goal, and have a mass of options when it comes down to attacking endeavour. However, they require a consistent goalscorer in the mould of Emilio Butragueño, who was a poacher of the highest order. The most likely person to fill this role is Raul Gonzalez. He could form a partnership with Real Betis' Alfonso who is wonderfully gifted with two quick feet and dazzling ball control. If the partnership works, Spain would finally prove to the footballing world what they are capable of.

LEFT: Luis Enrique Martinez playing in the 3-1 win against the Faroe Islands in October 1997.

ABOVE: Alfonso playing against Yugoslavia in the group qualifier in December 1996.

PLAYERS TO WATCH FOR

Fernando Hierro
Raul
Luis Enrique
Ivan de la Peña

FIRST ROUND MATCHES

Date	Opponents	Venue
13.6	Nigeria	Nantes
19.6	Paraguay	Saint-Etienne
24.6	Bulgaria	Lens

ITALY

After such a disastrous Euro '96, Cesare Maldini, who replaced Arrigo Sacchi, will be aiming to restore some Italian pride following their first round exit. Under the guidance of Maldini (the father of Milan full-back Paolo) the Italian U-21 side experienced continued successas he led them to a number of international triumphs. Despite Sacchi's failure in the European Championships, two years earlier he had steered the Azzuri to the World Cup Final in Pasadena. This was masterminded by the precocious talent of Roberto Baggio, who crafted some virtuoso performances. 'Il divino' is unlikely to be in France in '98, but in replacements Gianfranco Zola and Alessandro Del Piero, they have two able lieutenants. Zola produced rare glimpses of form during Euro '96, but has conjured up some breathtaking exhibitions following his move to Chelsea. With his guile, genius and ability to carve open the tight-

WORLD CUP HISTORY
Previous finals: 1934, 1938, 1950, 1954, 1962, 1966, 1970, 1974, 1978, 1982, 1986, 1990, 1994
Best performance: Winners 1934, 1938, 1982

EUROPE GROUP 2

TEAM	P	W	D	L	G	PTS
England	8	6	1	1	15–2	19
Italy	**8**	**5**	**3**	**0**	**11–1**	**18**
Poland	8	3	1	4	10–12	10
Georgia	8	3	1	4	7–9	10
Moldova	8	0	0	8	2–21	0

THE ROAD TO FRANCE

5.10.96	Moldova	(a)	1-3 (w)	10.9.97	Georgia	(a)	0-0 (d)
9.10.96	Georgia	(h)	1-0 (w)	11.10.97	England	(h)	0-0 (d)
12.2.97	England	(a)	0-1 (w)				
29.3.97	Moldova	(h)	3-0 (w)	**Play-offs**			
2.4.97	Poland	(a)	0-0 (d)	29.10.97	Russia	(a)	1-1 (d)
30.4.97	Poland	(h)	3-0 (w)	15.11.97	Russia	(h)	1-0 (w)

est of defences, could Zola be the key to Italian success? The men given the task of making the most of Zola's promptings are a selection of strikers with a degree of varying styles and qualities. If Maldini is looking for a more direct route to goal he need look no further than Lazio's Pier Luigi Casiraghi or Fabrizio Ravanelli of Marseille: both know the avenue to goal and have supplied goals during qualification — Casiraghi claiming the all important strike in Naples which finally sent the Azzuri to France. A fresher line of attack would bring a number of younger frontmen into the frame — Christain Vieri (now in Spain with Atletico Madrid), the largely untried Filipo Inzaghi and the 'new Paolo Rossi' Enrico Chiesa. With both Zola and Del Piero able to move from the floating role into more prominent positions, Maldini certainly has a host of options to call upon.

Previous Italian sides of quality have set their foundations on an impenetrable back line (the standard back four being the most deployed formation). Past masters have included Scirea,

ABOVE LEFT: The Italian team before the 30 April 1997 3-0 victory over Poland.

BELOW: Gianfranco Zola playing against England in October 1997.

Baresi, Gentile and Facchetti, with the current crop revolving around the elegant Paolo Maldini, Parma's Fabio Cannavaro, the erratic Alessandro Costacurta and the hard-nosed Ciro Ferrara. On occasion Maldini has experimented with the popular wing-back system, with Angelo Di Livio, Antonio Benarrivo and Alessandro Nesta occupying those positions. This defensive stability has been emphasised with Italy conceding only one goal in the group stages of qualification. For all their vigilance in defence, the lack of goals nearly cost Italy dear: failing to score in Poland and Georgia left Italy needing a victory in their final contest versus England in Rome. Once again Zola and co failed to create that goalscoring spark, leaving them to face the prospect of a hostile trip to Russia in a two-leg play-off. A combative one-all draw was followed by a scrappy one-nil victory at the San Paolo, an indication of Italy's ability to grind out victories when up against it. This, however, can be seen as a trait which has been absent from previous Italian sides, pointing the finger at the Italian temperament, which can be frustrating and non-motivational when their backs are against the wall. If Maldini can instil a fighting spirit, cohesion and consistency into Italy's play, they could well return to former glories, recreating the triumphs of Vittorio Pozzo (1934, 1938) and Enzo Bearzot in 1982.

Could Papa Maldini go one better this time and lead Italy to a fourth World Cup triumph?

ABOVE: Paolo Maldini playing in the 3-0 win against Poland in April 1997.

LEFT: Demetrio Albertini playing in the 1-0 victory against Russia in November 1997.

PLAYERS TO WATCH FOR

Paolo Maldini

Gianfranco Zola

Demetrio Albertini

FIRST ROUND MATCHES

Date	Opponents	Venue
11.6	Chile	Bordeaux
17.6	Cameroon	Montpellier
23.6	Austria	Saint-Denis

ROMANIA

Following their impressive qualification to France, Romania could prove to be a formidable presence at the World Cup as one of the eight seeded teams. The team is piloted once again by the authoritative Anghel Iordanescu, who had previously guided them to a magnificent quarter final place in 1994 (before losing on penalties to Sweden); he also directed them to Euro '96, where again good fortune was not on their side. Romania failed to record a victory, and to add insult to injury were deprived of victory against Bulgaria, when a goal-bound effort clearly crossed the line — the goal was not given and this effectively eliminated Romania from the tournament.

Putting frustration behind them, Romania showed convincing form during the qualifying campaign; Iordanescu's side won their first

WORLD CUP HISTORY
Previous finals: 1930, 1934, 1938, 1970, 1974, 1978, 1982, 1986, 1990, 1994
Best performance: Quarter finals 1994

EUROPE GROUP 8

TEAM	P	W	D	L	G	PTS
Romania	10	9	1	0	37-4	28
Rep of Ireland	10	5	3	2	22-8	18
Lithuania	10	5	2	3	11-8	17
Macedonia	10	4	1	5	22-18	13
Iceland	10	2	3	5	11-16	9
Liechtenstein	10	0	0	10	3-52	0

THE ROAD TO FRANCE

31.8.96	Lithuania	(h) 3-0 (w)		30.4.97	Rep Ireland	(h) 1-0 (w)
9.10.96	Iceland	(a) 0-4 (w)		20.8.97	Macedonia	(h) 4-2 (w)
14.12.96	Macedonia	(a) 0-3 (w)		6.9.97	Liechtenstein	(a) 1-8 (w)
29.3.97	Liechtenstein	(h) 8-0 (w)		10.9.97	Iceland	(h) 4-0 (w)
2.4.97	Lithuania	(a) 0-1 (w)		11.10.97	Rep Ireland	(a) 1-1 (d)

eight games, before recording a draw in the final tie. Goalscoring proved little obstacle for a rampant team, which recorded a mammoth 37 goals, while conceding just four. Romania swept every opponent they met aside, trouncing bewildered Liechtenstein 8-0 and 8-1, beating Iceland 4-0 twice and registering convincing victories over their remaining group opponents. If they should continue this form, and reproduce the tidy football displayed in the USA, they could be a serious contender for a semifinal place.

The foundation for recent Romanian achievement may well stem from the inspiring Steaua Bucharest side which conquered Europe in 1986, for whom Iordanescu was an integral part of the playing staff. The pivotal point of Iordanescu's squad is the enigmatic Gheorge Hagi, who earns his corn with Galatassary in Turkey. His guile and craft saw him voted as one of the tournament's top players in USA '94. Gifted with incredible vision and passing skills, he masterminded their passage to the quarter

ABOVE LEFT: The Romanian team that beat Liechtenstein 8-1 in the group qualifier.

BELOW: Dan Petrescu playing in the rout of Liechtenstein in September 1997.

finals. Nicknamed the 'Maradona of the Carpathians', can Romania's most influential figure inspire them to greater heights?

He will be aided by an array of varying talents, both defensive and offensive. These include Espanyol striker Florin Raducioiu, who scored four times in 1994; although his form tends to fluctuate and he is easily disheartened, when on song he can prove a real match winner. Further goals may revolve around striker Viorel Moldovan and the younger Adrian Ilie. Given the task of providing the ammunition for the front men will be another player who has experienced World Cup success — Ilie Dumitrescu who has plied his trade in Spain, England and even Mexico.

A further aspect of the Romanian team are the foraging runs by their full backs, in this case Dan Petrescu (in England with Chelsea) and Tiblr Selymes who plays in Belgium with Anderlecht. Both enjoy the attacking side of their work, often supplying goal scoring chances for their team mates. Concentrating on the more defensive side of the back line will be Atletico Madrid's Daniel Prodan and the elegant Gica Popescu who can also fill a midfield role when required. Both members of this defensive pairing are extremely comfortable on the ball and cool under pressure. They will provide a sound foundation on which to build.

As a seeded nation Romania should encounter few problems in progressing to the knock-out stages, and if the old guard of '94 can gel once more, they could be a team to watch.

ABOVE: Viorel Moldovan playing in the 8-1 win against Liechtenstein in September 1997.

LEFT: Gheorge Hagi before the Ireland game, October 1997.

PLAYERS TO WATCH FOR

Gheorge Hagi

Dan Petrescu

Viorel Moldovan

FIRST ROUND MATCHES

Date	Opponents	Venue
15.6	Colombia	Lyon
22.6	England	Toulouse
26.6	Tunisia	Saint-Denis

ARGENTINA

As twice World Champions the Argentine school of 1998 will be looking to recreate the success experienced by the side of 1978 (as host nation) and the Maradona-fuelled party in 1986. With a relatively poor showing in the USA, Batistuta et al will be hoping to restore some Argentine pride, and go beyond the second phase.

The skipper in 1978, Daniel Passarella, is the man given the task to reproduce the sort of form for which Argentina are recognised. He was instated just after the World Cup in the USA, and was in charge for Argentina's attempts to win the Copa America (a tournament which they have won on 14 occasions, the last being in 1993).

Minus Maradona, the squad is now mainly focused around a younger breed of players,

WORLD CUP HISTORY
Previous finals: 1930, 1934, 1958, 1962, 1966, 1974, 1978, 1982, 1986, 1990, 1994
Best performance: Winners 1978, 1986

SOUTH AMERICAN GROUP

TEAM	P	W	D	L	G	PTS
Argentina	16	8	6	2	23-13	30
Paraguay	16	9	2	5	21-14	29
Colombia	16	8	4	4	23-15	28
Chile	16	7	4	5	32-18	25
Peru	16	7	4	5	19-20	25
Ecuador	16	6	3	7	22-21	21
Uruguay	16	6	3	7	18-21	21
Bolivia	16	4	5	7	18-21	17
Venezuela	16	0	3	13	8-41	3

THE ROAD TO FRANCE

24.4.96	Bolivia	(h)	3-1 (w)	2.4.97	Bolivia	(a)	2-1 (l)
2.6.96	Ecuador	(a)	2-0 (l)	30.4.97	Ecuador	(h)	2-1 (w)
7.7.96	Peru	(a)	0-0 (d)	8.6.97	Peru	(h)	2-0 (w)
1.9.96	Paraguay	(h)	1-1 (d)	6.7.97	Paraguay	(a)	1-2 (w)
9.9 96	Venezuela	(a)	2-5 (w)	20.7.97	Venezuela	(h)	2-0 (w)
15.12.96	Chile	(h)	1-1 (d)	10.9.97	Chile	(a)	1-2 (w)
12.1.97	Uruguay	(a)	0-0 (d)	12.10.97	Uruguay	(h)	0-0 (d)
12.2.97	Columbia	(a)	0-1 (w)	16.11.97	Columbia	(h)	1-1 (d)

although some of the older and wiser heads still remain. Defenders Roberto Sensini and Jose Charmot have both participated in previous World Cup campaigns and will be able to support the less experienced team members. The up and coming talents within the national side include the devilish skills of Arnaldo Ortega, who plays in Spain with Valencia. His quick feet, speed of thought and incredible ball skills will surely see him emerge as one of the stars in France. It is likely that he will be accompanied in midfield by Juan Sebastian Veron — another whose career is currently flourishing in Europe, with Sampdoria in Italy. His pinpoint passing will aid Ortega's attempts to supply ammunition for their strikers. Stability will be provided by the influential Diego Simeone (Internazionale of Milan), whose powerful play and surging forays, as well as his tough tackling and tenacity, will cause many a problem for opponents.

ABOVE LEFT: The Argentine team that lost to Bolivia 2-1 in the group match of 2 April 1997.

BELOW: Gabriel Batistuta playing against Bulgaria in the 1994 World Cup.

Argentina will also welcome back Gabriele Batistuta, so long overlooked following disputes with the management. His forceful attacking play will surely reap rewards, especially when the supply will be delivered by Ortega and Veron. Batigol's main strengths lie in his aerial prowess and thunderous shooting (he managed four goals in the '94 tournament, including a hat-trick against Greece). The foil to Batistuta's powerful approach will be chosen from two younger strikers — Herman Crespo and Claudio Lopez, both in their early twenties, both would relish the chance to play a part in leading Argentina's front line in France.

The job of safeguarding any advantages that Argentina gain will be goalkeeper Carlos Roa (a newcomer to the international scene). He will be assisted by the uncompromising Sensini and Chamot, with Roberto Ayala completing a solid central trio.

If Passarella can get the best from his players, they could possibly return to past glories; but should Argentina experience early setbacks, will they have spirit to recover? That remains to be seen, but in players such as Ortega and Simeone they should progress further than the group stages.

ABOVE: Arnaldo Ortega playing in the 2-0 victory over Peru, 8 June 1997.

LEFT: Diego Simeone in action against Peru on 8 June 1997.

PLAYERS TO WATCH FOR

Arnaldo Ortega
Diego Simeone
Juan Sebastian Veron

FIRST ROUND MATCHES

Date	Opponents	Venue
14.6	Japan	Toulouse
21.6	Jamaica	Paris
26.6	Croatia	Bordeaux

HOLLAND

With the days of 'total football' a now fading memory, the class of '98 will be hoping to return to the days of Cruyff, Neeskens and Krol. It has been 10 years since a Dutch national side lifted a major international trophy. Their success at the European Championships in 1988 is amazingly the only silverware gained by a country with such proud footballing traditions. That was the side which contained the Milan trio of Gullit, Rijkaard and van Basten, as well as the Koeman brothers, Arnold Muhren and Gerald Vanenburg.

The new breed of Dutch stars revolves around Kluivert, Seedorf, Bergkamp and the De Boer twins. Could a trait of a successful Dutch national side revolve around having a set of brothers in your squad? The van der Kerkhoff twins in the 1970s, the Koemans in the 1980s — could the de Boers inspire the Dutch in France? Both are blessed with superb natural abilities, both are great readers of the game, both are accomplished at set plays and both

WORLD CUP HISTORY
Previous finals: 1934, 1954, 1974, 1978, 1990, 1994
Best performance: 2nd 1974, 1978

EUROPE GROUP 7

TEAM	P	W	D	L	G	PTS
Holland	8	6	1	1	26-4	19
Belgium	8	6	0	2	20-11	18
Turkey	8	4	2	2	21-9	14
Wales	8	2	1	5	20-21	7
San Marino	8	0	0	8	0-42	0

THE ROAD TO FRANCE

5.10.96	Wales	(a)	1-3 (w)	2.4.97	Turkey	(a)	1-0 (l)
9.11.96	Wales	(h)	7-1 (w)	30.4.97	San Marino	(a)	0-6 (w)
14.12.96	Belgium	(a)	0-3 (w)	6.9.97	Belgium	(h)	3-1 (w)
29.3.97	San Marino	(h)	4-0 (w)	11.10.97	Turkey	(h)	0-0 (d)

can provide crucial goals. Ronald is the more attack-minded of the pair, able to play in midfield or in a more forward role, while Frank plies his trade as a defender. The duo both come from the Ajax production line, as do so many of Holland's more gifted performers, whose flexibility is instilled in the Ajax schooling system. Ajax believe that every player should be able to perform well in every possible playing position: this approach has enabled Holland to create a versatile team formation.

The Dutch side is prominently made up from the two major Dutch club sides — Ajax and PSV Eindhoven. Added to this are the players who earn their keep overseas. Although today they playing in foreign leagues, their skills were honed at these two great clubs. Prime examples include Patrick Kluivert and Edgar Davids at Milan, Clarence Seedorf and Michael Reiziger in Spain with Real Madrid and Barcelona respectively, and the Arsenal duo of Marc Overmars and Dennis Bergkamp. Bergkamp (named Dennis after the great Denis Law) has

ABOVE LEFT: The Dutch team that demolished Wales 7-1 in their group qualifier in November 1996.

BELOW: Dennis Bergkamp celebrates during the win against Wales .

been a revelation at Highbury, and most of Holland's attacking ambitions will rest with him; he will be assisted with the goalscoring duties by the inconsistent Patrick Kluivert and up and coming Boujedwijn Zenden at PSV.

However, not all is rosy in the Dutch camp: the national side has been rife with conflict involving both players and the manager. Squabbles over playing staff, bonuses and team selection have been in abundance in recent years. Coach Juust Hiddink will be hoping that they put their differences aside, and furnish the Dutch with their first triumph in the World Cup. Holland's laid-back attitude maybe another flaw in their game, but this coolness can also work in their favour, with stars such as Overmars, Cocu, Seedorf and Ronald de Boer providing the opportunities for Bergkamp, they will not be short of goals. The stability will be provided by versatile Wim Jonk, the mighty Arthur Numan and newcomer Jaap Stam, all of whom are with PSV Eindhoven.

If the carefree nature gels with the stability and effectiveness in forward areas, there is no reason why Holland should not lift the World Cup in Paris in the summer. Or will the Dutch prove once again to be World Cup bridesmaids as in 1974 and 1978?

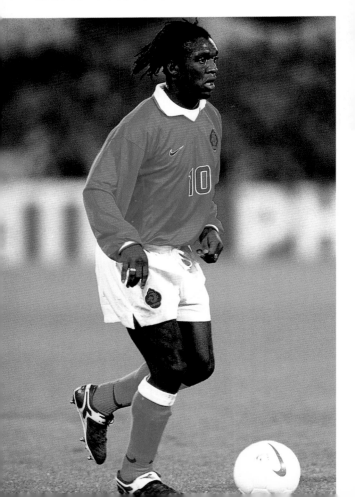

ABOVE: Ronald de Boer wheels away from the Welsh goal in November 1996.

LEFT: Clarence Seedorf during the 5 September qualifier against Belgium. Holland won 3-1.

PLAYERS TO WATCH FOR

Dennis Bergkamp
Ronald de Boer
Frank de Boer
Clarence Seedorf

FIRST ROUND MATCHES

Date	Opponents	Venue
13.6	Belgium	Saint-Denis
20.6	South Korea	Marseille
25.6	Mexico	Saint-Etienne

ENGLAND

Following England's success during the European Championships under the guidance of Terry Venables, the pressure was on Glenn Hoddle to build on the foundations of what Venables had started. The former Chelsea manager did so both by bringing in fresh new talent and also by keeping the best of the established stars.

Faced with some awkward looking adventures to Eastern Europe, Hoddle's side performed efficiently and achieved the desired results. With just one defeat in the qualifying games (against Italy at Wembley, a match which saw England deprived of a number of influential members of the squad), they finished as group winners, and claimed their place in France following their absence from USA '94 — an omission which would see England unseeded in France. England's passage was completed with a tremendous performance in the lion's den of Rome's Olympic Stadium, a sound defensive display helping them gain a deserved draw which left the Italians facing the lottery of a play-off.

World Cup History
Previous finals: 1950, 1954, 1958, 1962, 1966, 1970, 1982, 1986, 1990
Best performance: Winners 1966

EUROPE GROUP 2

TEAM	P	W	D	L	G	PTS
England	8	6	1	1	15-2	19
Italy	8	5	3	0	11-1	18
Poland	8	3	1	4	10-12	10
Georgia	8	3	1	4	7-9	10
Moldova	8	0	0	8	2-21	0

THE ROAD TO FRANCE

1.9.96	Moldova	(a)	0-3 (w)	30.4.97	Georgia	(h)	2-0 (w)
9.10.96	Poland	(h)	2-1 (w)	31.5.97	Poland	(a)	0-2 (w)
9.11.96	Georgia	(a)	0-2 (w)	10.9.97	Moldova	(h)	4-0 (w)
12.2.97	Italy	(h)	0-1 (l)	11.10.97	Italy	(a)	0-0 (d)

The main cause of England's triumphs was the defence — an impregnable back four or a back three with attacking wing-backs. The pivotal point of this solid foundation came in the form of goalkeeper David Seaman, rated by many as the world's finest. The Arsenal keeper shone during Euro '96 producing vital saves, none more so than during the penalty shoot-out with Spain in round two. Hoddle has an abundance of experience and youth to form a formidable barrier. Older heads such as Tony Adams and Gareth Southgate, and the new breed — the Neville brothers, Rio Ferdinand, Sol Campbell and the under-rated Chris Perry at Wimbledon. With the blooming wing-back formation Hoddle can call upon Graeme Le

ABOVE LEFT: England's team in training at Mottram Hall in May 1997.

BELOW: Alan Shearer playing against Georgia in the 2-0 win in April 1997.

Saux and Andy Hinchcliffe (along with the Neville brothers) to supply further ammunition for England's strikers

While England's main foundations stem from keeping it 'water tight' in defence, Hoddle can rely on a number of attacking options. If Shearer can fully recover after serious injury and stay fit, the only dilemma facing Hoddle could be who will partner the £15 million man. Hoddle has experimented with varying alternatives in Shearer's absence — two out and out strikers, or one lone striker with a further player droping in behind. This proved England's most fruitful tactic with Shearer and Sheringham forming a formidable duo. During Shearer's absence Hoddle has called upon the rejuvenated Ian Wright, Liverpool goal machine Robbie Fowler, Spurs' Les Ferdinand and, of course, Sheringham. However the newest ace in Hoddle's pack has been the presence of flame-haired terrier Paul Scholes; the Manchester United dynamo has shown maturity beyond his years with some commanding performances. This was emphasised on Scholes' scoring debut during England's Le Tournoi victory, where Hoddle's troops faced stern competition in the midsummer warm up.

Balanced with England's wealth of talent in

ABOVE: David Seaman playing against Italy in England's 0-0 draw in Rome, October 1997.

BELOW LEFT: A bandaged Paul Ince playing against Italy in Rome, October 1997.

attack and defence, they can also call upon workrate and stability in midfield, with Paul Ince and David Batty, coupled with the more subtle promptings of David Beckham, Steve McManaman, Jamie Redknapp and the revitalised Paul Gascoigne — back in the sort of form which he displayed during Italia '90.

If the nation can get behind England, and recreate the euphoria which swept over everyone during Euro '96, could the country which brought the football to the world, take something back? Will the Three Lions be roaring in France next summer?

PLAYERS TO WATCH FOR

Alan Shearer (if fit)

David Beckham

Paul Scholes

Sol Campbell

FIRST ROUND MATCHES

Date	Opponents	Venue
15.6	Tunisia	Marseille
22.6	Romania	Toulouse
26.6	Colombia	Lens

NORWAY

Once again Norway has qualified for the World Cup Finals — the second time in succession — ahead of bigger countries. Under the watchful eye of master tactician Egil Olsen, they have proved again that they are Europe's fastest developing football nation. The foundation for Norway's growing ability to 'rub people's noses in it', is the team's fitness, hard work and flexibility — the same reasons so many of the English Premiership's top teams opt for Norwegian imports: over half of Norway's probable squad ply their trade in British football.

A prime example of these traits is Liverpool midfielder Oyvind Leonhardsen, who made his name at Rosenberg, where he was Norway's footballer of the year two years in succession. He moved to England and Wimbledon, before joining Liverpool, where he combines his tireless work rate and tenacity with sublime skills.

Norway does not just boast a side of battlers: players such as Stalle Solbakken, Stig Inge Bjornebye and Petter Rudi are genuine stars. However, the figure upon whom most eyes will be focused is Manchester United's baby-faced

World Cup History
Previous finals: 1938, 1994
Best performance: 1st round

EUROPE GROUP 3

TEAM	P	W	D	L	G	PTS
Norway	8	6	2	0	21-2	20
Hungary	8	3	3	2	10-8	12
Finland	8	3	2	3	11-12	11
Switzerland	8	3	1	4	11-12	10
Azerbaijan	8	1	0	7	3-22	3

THE ROAD TO FRANCE

2.6.96	Azerbaijan	(h)	5-0 (w)	8.6.97	Hungary	(a)	1-1 (d)
9.10.96	Hungary	(h)	3-0 (w)	20.8.97	Finland	(a)	0-4 (w)
10.11.96	Switzerland	(a)	0-1 (w)	6.9.97	Azerbaijan	(a)	0-1 (w)
30.4.97	Finland	(h)	1-1 (d)	10.9.97	Switzerland	(h)	5-0 (w)

assassin: Ole Gunnar Solskjaer, a young man who is already a deadly threat to defences throughout Europe, and United's leading marksmen during the 1996-97 season.

Although Norway gained few fans following their dour displays during the World Cup four years ago, their new-found attacking prowess could see them progress beyond the preliminary group stages for the first time.

What the side lacks is a real on-field general or schemer— like Djorkaeff for the French or Haessler for the Germans. This lack of someone who can change a game, could be their downfall — but they will go down battling.

PLAYERS TO WATCH FOR

Ole Gunnar Solskjaer
Oyvind Leonhardsen
Stig Inge Bjornebye

FIRST ROUND MATCHES

Date	Opponents	Venue
10.6	Morocco	Montpellier
16.6	Scotland	Bordeaux
23.6	Brazil	Marseille

ABOVE LEFT: The Norwegian team that beat Finland 4-0 in August 1997.

BELOW: Stig Inge Bjornebye playing against Finland in August 1997.

BULGARIA

Bulgaria's display in USA '94 raised eyebrows all around the footballing world as their shock passage to the semi-finals saw them dispose of then reigning champions West Germany, only for the adventure to end with defeat by a Baggio-inspired Italian side. This incredible form was even more surprising following their drubbing by Nigeria in their opening fixture. The coach, Dimitar Penev, has since been replaced by Hristo Bonev (shortly after Bulgaria's first round exit in Euro '96).

Bulgaria's continued success in qualifying for major tournaments has centred around the squad's stability and cohesion. Sticking to a conventional 4-4-2 formation, they have experimented little in their tactical plans. The key influence has been the mastery of the temperamental Hristo Stoichkov, joint leading marksmen in 1994 with six goals. His cunning and guile can turn a game in an instant, such as his free-kick in the victory over Germany four years previous. At 31, Stoichkov can still conjure up moments of genius, although he has seen little

World Cup History
Previous finals: 1962, 1966, 1970, 1974, 1986, 1994
Best performance: 4th place 1994

EUROPE GROUP 5

TEAM	P	W	D	L	G	PTS
Bulgaria	**8**	**6**	**0**	**2**	**18-9**	**18**
Russia	8	5	2	1	19-5	17
Israel	8	4	1	3	9-7	13
Cyprus	8	3	1	4	10-15	10
Luxembourg	8	0	0	8	2-22	0

THE ROAD TO FRANCE

1.9.96	Israel	(a)	2-1 (l)	8.6.97	Luxembourg	(h)	4-0 (w)
8.10.96	Luxembourg	(a)	1-2 (w)	20.8.97	Israel	(h)	1-0 (w)
14.12.96	Cyprus	(a)	1-3 (w)	10.9.97	Russia	(h)	1-0 (w)
2.4.97	Cyprus	(h)	4-1 (w)	11.10.97	Russia	(a)	4-2 (l)

first team football over the past few seasons with Parma in Serie A and Spanish giants Barcelona. Complementing the enigmatic Stoichkov, is the bustling target man, 30-year old Emil Kostadinov. Spain-based striker Luboslav Penev could also see some action if Stoichkov and Kostadinov fail to deliver.

The periphery of the Bulgarian squad consists of a collection of experienced footballing journey men. The silky Krassimir Balakov, who plays in Germany with Stuttgart, the efficient Zlatko Ivanov, Rapid Vienna's tough-tackling man-marker Trifon Ivanov and, of course, the balding Yordan Letchkov (a cult figure in the USA '94). Bulgaria's qualification was comparatively straightforward from an awkward qualifying stage consisting of Russia, Israel, Cyprus, and Luxembourg. The Bulgarian ethic of work rate, tenacity and efficiency, a common trait amongst many Eastern European nations, should see them advance to the later stages as in 1994. Their commitment and resilience coupled with their obvious talents could see them once again labelled as tournament dark horses.

ABOVE LEFT: The Bulgarian team that beat Russia 1-0 in Sofia 10 September 1997.

BELOW: Hristo Stoichkov playing against Russia.

PLAYERS TO WATCH FOR

Hristo Stoichkov
Krassimir Balakov

FIRST ROUND MATCHES

Date	Opponents	Venue
12.6	Paraguay	Montpellier
19.6	Nigeria	Paris
24.6	Spain	Lens

MEXICO

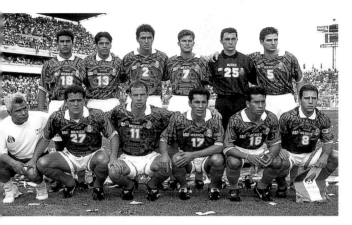

Mexico are setting out their 11th World Cup adventure. Now back under the guidance of Bora Milutinovic (he led them to the quarter finals in 1986; they lost to West Germany on penalties), they hope to progress even further. 'Bora' is an experienced national coach: this is his fourth successive appearance in the World Cup finals, having been there previously with Mexico, Costa Rica — who reached the second phase in Italia '90 (including a shock victory over Scotland) — and in 1994 the USA, whom he took beyond the group stages.

The wily Serbian has based his squads around a willingness to win, attacking flair and team spirit. The 1998 Mexican side is no exception, and Milutinovic's selections will revolve around invigorating attacking play, an experienced midfield and a unique Mexican exuberance. Leading this colourful assault will be eccentric goalkeeper Jorge Campos, renowned for his neon jerseys and tendency to be seen

World Cup History
Previous finals: 1930, 1950, 1954, 1958, 1962, 1966, 1970, 1978, 1986, 1994
Best performance: Quarter finals 1970, 1986

CONCACAF GROUP

TEAM	P	W	D	L	G	PTS
Mexico	**10**	**4**	**6**	**0**	**23-7**	**18**
United States	10	4	5	1	17-9	17
Jamaica	10	3	5	2	7-12	14
Costa Rica	10	3	3	4	13-12	12
El Salvador	10	2	4	4	11-16	11
Canada	10	1	3	6	5-18	6

THE ROAD TO FRANCE

2.3.97	Canada	(h)	4-0 (w)	5.10.97	El Salvador	(h)	5-0 (w)
16.3.97	Costa Rica	(a)	0-0 (d)	12.10.97	Canada	(a)	2-2 (d)
13.4.97	Jamaica	(h)	6-0 (w)	2.11.97	USA	(h)	0-0 (d)
20.4.97	USA	(a)	2-2 (d)	9.11.97	Costa Rica	(h)	3-3 (d)
8.6.97	El Salvador	(a)	0-1 (w)	16.11.97	Jamaica	(a)	0-0 (d)

outside his own penalty area, sometimes even as a striker, although his goalkeeping position has been taken by Aldolfo Rios recently.

Goal scoring proved no obstacle for Mexico in the qualifying stages from the CONCACAF section: they scored 20 times, conceded just four and were unbeaten. The main weight of their attacking options falls on the shoulders of three contrasting strikers: Luis Garcia, supremely gifted and a star in 1994, the lightning fast Luis Hernandez and Alves Zague, all of whom are capable of consistently finding the net.

The ammunition will be supplied by an ageing midfield of Ben Galindo, Alberto Coyote and Luis Garcia Aspe, whose experience could prove invaluable if Mexico are to go beyond the group stages. If they can reproduce the sort of form showed in the Copa America tournaments of 1993 (finalists) and 1997 (semi-finalists), they could well improve on their display in the USA.

ABOVE LEFT: The Mexican team due to play against Costa Rica in March 1997.

BELOW: Luis Hernandez playing against Ecuador in the 4-3 win in June 1997.

PLAYERS TO WATCH FOR

Luis Hernandez
Pavel Pardo

FIRST ROUND MATCHES

Date	Opponents	Venue
13.6	South Korea	Lyon
20.6	Belgium	Bordeaux
25.6	Holland	Saint-Etienne

JAMAICA

The new rhythm in France next year will be supplied by 'The Reggae Boyz' of Jamaica, participating in their first World Cup finals. The team and followers will bring a new wave of colour to the tournament, as well as different face to the world stage. Following a shaky start to their qualification campaign, Jamaica recovered to earn valuable results against bigger nations. Qualification was finally guaranteed by a gritty draw with group winners Mexico, after which a national holiday was declared by Prime Minister Percival Patterson.

Led by Brazilian coach Rene Simoes, the Jamaicans played a total of 20 matches to reach France, conceding more goals than they scored. As this record suggests, Jamaica's playing style revolves more around attack than defence — an approach owing much to coach Simoes who first took over in 1994. The attacking strategies have tended to revolve around the new influx of players recruited from English sides, none more so than Derby County striker Deon Burton, who

World Cup History
First appearance in finals

CONCACAF GROUP

TEAM	P	W	D	L	G	PTS
Mexico	10	4	6	0	23-7	18
United States	10	4	5	1	17-9	17
Jamaica	**10**	**3**	**5**	**2**	**7-12**	**14**
Costa Rica	10	3	3	4	13-12	12
El Salvador	10	2	4	4	11-16	11
Canada	10	1	3	6	5-18	6

THE ROAD TO FRANCE

2.3.97	USA	(h)	0-0 (d)	7.9.97	Canada	(h)	1-0 (w)
13.4.97	Mexico	(a)	6-0 (l)	14.9.97	Costa Rica	(h)	1-0 (w)
20.4.97	Canada	(a)	0-0 (d)	3.10.97	USA	(a)	1-1 (d)
11.5.97	Costa Rica	(a)	3-1 (l)	9.11.97	El Salvador	(a)	2-2 (d)
18.5.97	El Salvador	(h)	1-0 (w)	16.11.97	Mexico	(h)	0-0 (d)

scored a vital equaliser in the 1—1 away draw with the US. Alongside Burton, Jamaica have welcomed Robbie Earle of Wimbledon and Portsmouth duo Fitzroy Simpson and Paul Hall, and the number of UK-based players wishing to represent Jamaica is increasing. With a firm emphasis on attack the recent form of the defence should not be overlooked — they kept six clean sheets in the latter stages of qualification, despite conceding six against Mexico in one of the earlier ties.

The popularity of football in Jamaica was demonstrated with thousands of fans being locked out of the final group game, and spectators arriving at the national stadium four hours before kick-off. Although there is little likelihood that Jamaica will progress far in the tournament, two things are certain: players and fans will have a great time and France will enjoy welcoming them.

ABOVE LEFT: Jamaica about to play Mexico in November 1997.

BELOW: Robbie Earle playing against Mexico.

PLAYERS TO WATCH FOR

Deon Burton
Paul Hall
Robbie Earle

FIRST ROUND MATCHES

Date	Opponents	Venue
14.6	Croatia	Lens
21.6	Argentina	Paris
26.6	Japan	Lyon

CAMEROON

Who will ever forget Cameroon's mesmerising performances during Italia '90? The Roger Milla 'wiggle' at the corner flag following his every goal, the flamboyant fans or even the more cynical side to their game in the opening match against Argentina? The 'Indomitable Lions', as they became known, put up less of a spirited display in the USA four years later, failing to win a match, although that fresh-faced naivete still remained. This time around, under the watchful gaze of coach Jean Manga Onguene, they hope to establish themselves once more on the game's grandest arena. Onguene was Valeri Nepomniachi's assistant in 1990, and was appointed head coach in 1997. His aim is clearly to steer Cameroon to a better showing than in the USA. This will be aided by knowing that a number of his more influential squad members tasted competition four years earlier. These include youthful captain Rigobert Song — just 17 in 1994, the young central defender currently plays for top French side Metz. Other Cameroon players also earn their corn in more testing leagues around the world: goalkeeper Jaques Songolo plays for Deportivo La Coruna,

World Cup History
Previous finals: 1982, 1990, 1994
Best performance: Quarter finals 1990

AFRICA GROUP 4

TEAM	P	W	D	L	G	PTS
Cameroon	6	4	2	0	10-4	14
Angola	6	2	4	0	7-4	10
Zimbabwe	6	1	1	4	6-7	4
Togo	6	1	1	4	6-14	4

THE ROAD TO FRANCE

10.11.96	Togo	(a)	2-4 (w)	27.4.97	Togo	(h)	2-0 (w)
12.1.97	Angola	(h)	0-0 (d)	8.6.97	Angola	(a)	1-1 (d)
6.4.97	Zimbabwe	(h)	1-0 (w)	17.8.97	Zimbabwe	(a)	1-2 (w)

Pierre Wome in Italy's Serie A and front man Alphonse Tchami appeared for the legendary Boca Juniors in Argentina.

Although Cameroon qualified comfortably from the African section (topping their group, scoring 10 and conceding just four), lessons will need to be learned from previous world cup adventures. For all the Cameroonian exuberance, there is an air of naivete about their approach to matches, displayed by over zealous tackling which leads to countless disciplinary problems. If this side of their playing style can be curbed, they could raise a few eyebrows, because they certainly have some creative performers, such as defender Rigobert Song and the talented Marc Vivien Foe in central midfield. As always Cameroon will be a joy to watch and will bring a unique quality to France in the summer.

ABOVE LEFT: The Cameroon team that beat Zimbabwe 2-1 in their group match in August 1997.

BELOW: Patrick Mbuma playing against Zimbabwe in August 1997.

PLAYERS TO WATCH FOR

Rigobert Song
Patrick Mbomba

FIRST ROUND MATCHES

Date	Opponents	Venue
11.6	Austria	Toulouse
17.6	Italy	Montpellier
23.6	Chile	Nantes

SOUTH AFRICA >

The Bafana Bafana are set to embark on their first ever appearance in the World Cup finals, just two years after their first victory in the African Nations Championship, clinched with a 2–0 victory over Tunisia. The 'Rainbow Nation' qualified with ease from their African section, conceding only three goals in eight games, which included six clean sheets.

Clive Barker is the man responsible for their recent success. Taking the reins in 1994, he inspired them to major success in just two years following his take over as coach.

With the difficulties surrounding politics in South Africa during the apartheid years, sport had been left in the international wilderness. It should have left the sporting squads floundering behind the rest of Africa and the world, but this theory could not have been wider of the mark. When South African teams were accepted back into the international fold, they produced remarkable displays culminating with the Springboks winning Rugby's 1995 World Cup.

Now it's the turn of the Bafana to enhance their reputation in France. The team is made up of players from overseas leagues ranging from

World Cup History
First appearance in finals

AFRICA GROUP 3

TEAM	P	W	D	L	G	PTS
South Africa	**6**	**4**	**1**	**1**	**7-3**	**13**
Congo	6	3	1	2	5-5	10
Zambia	6	2	2	2	7-6	8
Zaire	6	0	2	4	4-9	2

THE ROAD TO FRANCE

8.11.96	Zaire	(h)	1-0 (w)	27.4.97	Zaire	(a)	1-2 (w)
11.1.97	Zambia	(a)	0-0 (d)	8.6.97	Zambia	(h)	3-0 (w)
6.4.97	Congo	(a)	2-0 (l)	17.8.97	Congo	(h)	1-0 (w)

Italy to the USA and England, a popular destination for several influential figures in the South African set up, such as central defenders Luca Radebe (Leeds) and the impressive Mark Fish at Bolton (a crowd favourite amongst the South African contingent who wave fish at matches as a sign of their esteem!). Tough tackling midfielder Eric Tinkler is in the north-east with Barnsley and goalkeeper Andre Arendse is currently at Fulham. South African players have adapted well in the English leagues, because of their determination and work rate, but they are not without more skilled practitioners such as the talented John 'Shoes' Moshoeu, the influential Doctor Khulmalo (who plays for the Columbus Crew in the USA's MSL) and the loping figure of Phil Masinga (at Bari in Italy's Serie A), who could be South Africa's goal scoring spearhead with his forceful style of play.

ABOVE LEFT: The South African team to play against Zambia in the group match of June 1997.

BELOW: Phil Masinga playing against Congo in August 1997.

PLAYERS TO WATCH FOR

John Moshoeu
Phil Masinga

FIRST ROUND MATCHES

Date	Opponents	Venue
12.6	France	Marseille
18.6	Denmark	Toulouse
24.6	Saudi Arabia	Bordeaux

USA

As hosts in 1994 the pressure was on the USA team: every country staging the finals had qualified for the second phase, and they had a tight group consisting of Colombia, Romania and Switzerland. Against all odds the USA progressed to the knock out phase, before finally succumbing to eventual winners Brazil. This brought soccer into the American spotlight and saw the formation of the Major Soccer League in 1996. This has so far proved a success, with a number of top South American stars and senior European professionals heading to the newly formed league.

Today the man attempting to improve on the USA's great efforts four years earlier is coach Steve Sampson, a member of Bora Milutinovic's coaching staff prior to the 1994 tournament.

The USA squad is a mixture of experienced professionals who have plied their trade in Europe — John Harkes in England, Eric Wynalda in Germany, Alexi Lalas in Italy's Serie

World Cup History
Previous finals: 1930, 1934, 1950, 1990, 1994
Best performance: Semi finals 1930

CONCACAF GROUP

TEAM	P	W	D	L	G	PTS
Mexico	10	4	6	0	23-7	18
United States	**10**	**4**	**5**	**1**	**17-9**	**17**
Jamaica	10	3	5	2	7-12	14
Costa Rica	10	3	3	4	13-12	12
El Salvador	10	2	4	4	11-16	11
Canada	10	1	3	6	5-18	6

THE ROAD TO FRANCE

2.3.97	Jamaica	(a)	0-0 (d)	7.9.97	Costa Rica	(h)	1-0 (w)
16.3.97	Canada	(a)	3-0 (l)	3.10.97	Jamaica	(h)	1-1 (d)
23.3.97	Costa Rica	(a)	3-2 (w)	2.11.97	Mexico	(a)	0-0 (d)
20.4.97	Mexico	(h)	2-2 (d)	9.11.97	Canada	(a)	0-3 (w)
1.5.97	El Salvador	(a)	1-1 (d)	16.11.97	El Salvador	(h)	4-2 (w)

A and Ernie Stewart who is still in the Dutch top flight. The framework for possible USA triumph lies in the team's spirit and will to win (a common ethic amongst most Americans). This is balanced with squad stability — everyone is seen as an equal and has great pride in representing their nation.

The USA side is not only based on good intentions and morale, they also have a number of genuinely gifted talents: goalkeepers Kasey Keller (Leicester City) and Brad Friedel have both shown outstanding ability as have defenders Marcelo Balboa and the eccentric Alexei Lalas; tenacity in midfield is provided by John Harkes and Thomas Dooley, and more subtle skills by Claudio Reyna and lightning fast Cobi Jones. The task of goal scoring lies firmly at the feet of Eric Wynalda and Ernie Stewart.

If they can overcome their inconsistent form, the USA could well make it to the second phase.

ABOVE LEFT: The US team that lost to Costa Rica in the group match of March 1997.

BELOW: John Harkes playing against El Salvador.

PLAYERS TO WATCH FOR

John Harkes
Eric Wynalda
Kasey Keller

FIRST ROUND MATCHES

Date	Opponents	Venue
15.6	Germany	Paris
21.6	Iran	Lyon
25.6	Yugoslavia	Nantes

TUNISIA

It has been 20 years since Tunisia last appeared at a World Cup finals: that was in the 1978 tournament hosted by Argentina. The main focus of praise for Tunisia's progression must be on Polish coach Henryk Kasperczak (once himself an accomplished star with the Poland national team of the 1970s), who has developed his coaching skills and styles in the French leagues. He has coached a number of teams in France including Metz, St. Etienne, Strasbourg, Montpellier, Lille and Matra. Kasperczak took the reins in 1994 following a spell with the Ivory Coast national side. He has ushered Tunisia through a testing qualifying campaign where they topped a group containing the George Weah-fuelled Liberia, Egypt, and an unknown quantity in Namibia (this followed a preliminary two-leg tie with Rwanda). Tunisia came through unscathed, and unbeaten, totalling a comfortable 10 goals and conceding only one. They displayed firm discipline and resolve in some of the more hazardous away fixtures.

The growing strength of the Tunisians was demonstrated in the African Nations

World Cup History
Previous finals: 1978
Best performance: 1st round 1978

AFRICA GROUP 2

TEAM	P	W	D	L	G	PTS
Tunisia	**6**	**5**	**1**	**0**	**10-1**	**16**
Egypt	6	3	1	2	15-5	10
Liberia	6	1	1	4	2-10	4
Namibia	6	1	1	4	6-17	4

THE ROAD TO FRANCE

10 11 96	Liberia	(a)	0-1 (w)	27.4.97	Liberia	(h)	2-0 (w)
12.1.97	Egypt	(h)	1-0 (w)	8.6.97	Egypt	(a)	0-0 (d)
6.4.97	Namibia	(a)	1-2 (w)	17.8.97	Namibia	(h)	4-0 (w)

Championship of 1996. They threatened to gate crash the South African-hosted party, and steal the Bafana Bafana's glory — but it was not to be; they finally succumbed 2–0 in the final. If they can build on their rising fortunes, they may cause a few upsets in France. The duo aiming to grab the headlines will be striking partnership of Adel Sellimi and Ben Slimane. Both are in their early 20s and looking for goals. Their enthusiasm and exuberance will no doubt put pressure on opposing rearguards. When combining this with the creativity of midfielders Zoubeir Beya, Riadh Bouazizi and Skandi Souyah, Tunisia could figure as Africa's most promising representatives in France.

The key will be to maintain their defensive stability. Central to this ideal will be goalkeeper Chokra El Ouaer and the solid Khaled Badra, who could be kept busy in one of the less well known nations of the World Cup.

ABOVE LEFT: The Tunisian team that played Liberia in April 1997.

BELOW: Skandi Souyah in action.

PLAYERS TO WATCH FOR

Adel Sellimi
Khaled Badra

FIRST ROUND MATCHES

Date	Opponents	Venue
15.6	England	Marseille
22.6	Colombia	Montpellier
26.6	Romania	Saint-Denis

DENMARK

Denmark last tasted World Cup football back in 1986. During that tournament the Danes produced some breathtaking football. They were able to field such talents as Preben Elkjaer, Jesper Olsen, Soren Lerby and Michael Laudrup, who has recently returned to the national side. He has lost none of his drive, dribbling ability and mesmeric ball skills. The Dane has experienced football at the highest level and will definitely be a welcomed asset to Bo Johansson's squad. Johansson has replaced Richard Moller-Nielsen as coach, and has reinstated Laudrup into the national fold. Johansson has a tough act to follow, for it was Moller-Nielsen who masterminded Denmark's finest hour in international football. As a late entrant to the European Championships they proceeded to knock-out holders Holland in the semi-finals, and caused a major upset by defeating then World Champions Germany in the final.

Denmark's last World Cup engagement saw them progress to the quarter finals. If they can repeat this, they will have exceeded expectations.

World Cup History
Previous finals: 1986
Best performance: 2nd round

EUROPE GROUP 1

TEAM	P	W	D	L	G	PTS
Denmark	8	5	2	1	**14-6**	17
Croatia	8	4	3	1	17-12	15
Greece	8	4	2	2	11-4	14
Bosnia	8	3	0	5	9-14	9
Slovenia	8	0	1	7	5-20	1

THE ROAD TO FRANCE

1.9.96	Slovenia	(a)	0-2 (w)	8.6.97	Bosnia	(h)	2-0 (w)
9.10.96	Greece	(h)	2-1 (w)	20.8.97	Bosnia	(a)	3-0 (l)
29.3.97	Croatia	(a)	1-1 (d)	10.9.97	Croatia	(h)	3-1 (w)
30.4.97	Slovenia	(h)	4-0 (w)	11.10.97	Greece	(a)	0-0 (d)

They performed well during qualification to top their group. The Danes' more effective displays tend to revolve around the cunning and craft of the brothers Laudrup. Laudrup the younger's game focuses on his quick feet, smart brain and his penetrating attacking surges. His goal scoring abilities can also be brought into the frame, a quality which sometimes eludes his older brother. The genius of the Laudrups should open up opportunities for their front men — Nikolas Molnar and Peter Moller, both of whom opt for a forceful style of play.

Apart from their obvious attacking options, Denmark can call upon possibly the world's finest goalkeeper — Peter Schmeichel, seen by many as football's most proficient shot stopper. In front of the 'Great Dane' are the colossal figures of Marc Rieper and Jes Hogh, further strengthening the solid rearguard.

ABOVE LEFT: Denmark's team that won 3-1 against Croatia in the group qualifier, September 1997.

BELOW: Brian Laudrup playing against Greece in their 0-0 draw in October 1997.

PLAYERS TO WATCH FOR

Peter Schmeichel
Michael and Brian Laudrup

FIRST ROUND MATCHES

Date	Opponents	Venue
12.6	Saudi Arabia	Lens
18.6	South Africa	Toulouse
24.6	France	Lyon

MOROCCO

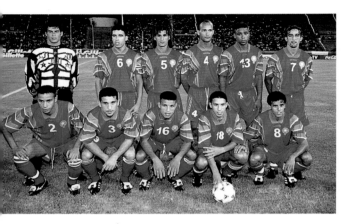

The Moroccans are set to embark on their fourth World Cup finals: they failed to impress during USA '94 where they did not win a match. Their performances in Mexico in 1986 were far better: they progressed to the second round, topping their table and then faced the might of West Germany. Despite putting up a spirited fight they lost to a solitary goal.

It will be vastly experienced coach Henri Michel who will oversee their assault on France. The Frenchman has tasted the World Cup as a player and coach on three previous occasions (two as coach). Prior endeavours were with the French national side (third place in 1986), Cameroon in USA '94 and as a player in 1978. Michel will be using his extensive knowledge to bring the best from his squad; he used his mastery to direct the French Olympic soccer team to a gold medal in LA in 1984.

The jewels in Henri Michel's crown are likely to be Noureddine Naybet, Ahmed Bahja and Moustafa Hadji. The talented Naybet will be at the heart of Morocco's defence, and aiming to continue the defensive record shown in qualifi-

World Cup History
Previous finals: 1970, 1986, 1994
Best performance: Second round 1986

AFRICA GROUP 5

TEAM	P	W	D	L	G	PTS
Morroco	**6**	**5**	**1**	**0**	**14-2**	**16**
Sierra Leone	5	2	1	2	4-6	7
Ghana	6	1	3	2	7-7	6
Gabon	5	0	1	4	1-11	1

THE ROAD TO FRANCE

9.11.96	Sierra-Leone	(h)	4-0 (w)	26.4.97	Sierra Leone	(a)	0-1 (w)
12.1.97	Ghana	(a)	2-2 (d)	7.6.97	Ghana	(h)	1-0 (w)
6.4.97	Gabon	(a)	4-0 (w)	17.8.97	Gabon	(h)	2-0 (w)

cation. Naybet will be seeking to recreate the form which saw him move to Spain's Primera Liga with Deportivo La Coruna. He will rely on his strength, guile and leadership qualities but despite this, goalkeeper Abdelkader El Brazi could be kept extremely busy and will need to be at his sharpest.

Morocco's key front runners are Ahmed Bahja, Moustafa El Hadji and Salaheddine Bassir. This trio will look to resume the goalscoring shown in qualification (14 goals in total). Bahja will call upon his height and dribbling abilities to cause problems for opponents; El Hadji looks to his elusiveness and pace; while Bassir will rely on his enthusiasm.

Their noisy fans will make themselves heard in France, and will hope their support can guide Morocco to greater achievements. However, despite this support, Morocco may find themselves on a early flight back to Rabat.

ABOVE LEFT: The Moroccan team that won their group qualifier against Gabon in August 1997.

BELOW: Salaheddine Bassir playing against Gabon in August 1997.

PLAYERS TO WATCH FOR

Noureddine Naybet
Ahmed Bahja

FIRST ROUND MATCHES

Date	Opponents	Venue
10.6	Norway	Montpellier
16.6	Brazil	Nantes
23.6	Scotland	Saint-Etienne

SCOTLAND

In France, Scotland will be looking to progress beyond the group stages for the first time in their eighth outing. They qualified as the best runner-up from the European section, finalised by a 2–0 victory over Latvia in their last game. Given the task of guiding Scotland past the first round will be the amiable Craig Brown, whose knowledge of tactical play and his enthusiastic approach to the game make him one of football's most popular coaches.

The Scottish style centres around the virtues of workrate, teamwork and passion, although they do possess some supremely gifted individuals. The Scots suffered only one defeat in the qualifying games and this is where Scotland's strengths lie; they managed to keep seven clean sheets, with dominating displays from Colin Hendry, Tom Boyd and Colin Calderwood. Manipulation of the defence has seen the development of the wing-back system, the positions

World Cup History
Previous finals: 1954, 1958, 1974, 1978, 1982, 1986, 1990, 1994
Best performance: 1st round

EUROPE GROUP 4

TEAM	P	W	D	L	G	PTS
Austria	10	8	1	1	17-4	25
Scotland	**10**	**7**	**2**	**1**	**15-3**	**23**
Sweden	10	7	0	3	16-9	21
Latvia	10	3	1	6	10-14	10
Estonia	10	1	1	8	4-16	4
Belarus	10	1	1	8	5-21	4

THE ROAD TO FRANCE

31.8.96	Austria	(a)	0-0 (d)	2.4.97	Austria	(h)	2-0 (w)
5.10.96	Latvia	(a)	0-2 (w)	30.4.97	Sweden	(a)	2-1 (l)
10.11.96	Sweden	(h)	1-0 (w)	8.6.97	Belarus	(a)	0-1 (w)
11.2.97	Estonia	(a)	0-0 (d)	7.9.97	Belarus	(h)	4-1 (w)
29.3.97	Estonia	(h)	2-0 (w)	11.10.97	Latvia	(h)	2-0 (w)

competently filled by Jackie McNamara, Craig Burley and Tosh McKinlay. Burley has also paraded his talents within the midfield. One midfield berth has been more frequently occupied by the masterly Gary McAllister, whose accurate long-range passing is a noticeable feature of his game. Alongside McAllister is the skilful John Collins, who plays his club football with Monaco in France. The developing capabilities of David Hopkin have provided a touch of steel to the central areas, with Paul Lambert as another able deputy.

It may be the lack of fire power which could hinder their aspirations. Kevin Gallagher has shown some impressive form for both club and country in 1997, and will hope to continue this. If they could find a man to hit the back of net with more regularity, they could progress to the second phase for the first time.

ABOVE LEFT: Scotland's team that won 3-2 against Malta in June 1997.

BELOW: Gary McAllister playing against Austria.

PLAYERS TO WATCH FOR

Gary McAllister
Kevin Gallagher

FIRST ROUND MATCHES

Date	Opponents	Venue
10.6	Brazil	Saint-Denis
16.6	Norway	Bordeaux
23.6	Morocco	Saint-Etienne

COLOMBIA

Headlines surrounding Colombia during the World Cup in 1994, were not focused on the team's on-field efforts, but off-field and the murder of defender Andreas Escoba. This time round, under coach Herman Dario Gomez, Columbia hopes to display a better class of football: there are certainly the talents within the squad to do so. One man who has been a key influence to Colombia's recent World Cup sorties is the unmistakeable Carlos Valderamma. His flamboyant skills have yet to be fully paraded on the World Cup stage, but he is quite capable of conjuring up moments of genius and slicing open any defence, although at 36 he is surely past his best. In recent seasons he has played for the Tampa Bay Mutiny in the USA's MSL.

World Cup History
Previous finals: 1962, 1990, 1994
Best performance: 2nd round

SOUTH AMERICAN GROUP

TEAM	P	W	D	L	G	PTS
Argentina	16	8	6	2	23-13	30
Paraguay	16	9	2	5	21-14	29
Colombia	**16**	**8**	**4**	**4**	**23-15**	**28**
Chile	16	7	4	5	32-18	25
Peru	16	7	4	5	19-20	25
Ecuador	16	6	3	7	22-21	21
Uruguay	16	6	3	7	18-21	21
Bolivia	16	4	5	7	18-21	17
Venezuela	16	0	3	13	8-41	3

THE ROAD TO FRANCE

24.4.96	Paraguay	(h)	1-0 (w)	2.4.97	Paraguay	(a)	2-1 (l)
2.6.96	Peru	(a)	1-1 (d)	30.4.97	Peru	(h)	0-1 (l)
7.7.96	Uruguay	(h)	3-1 (w)	8.6.97	Uruguay	(a)	1-1 (d)
1.9.96	Chile	(h)	4-1 (w)	5.7.97	Chile	(a)	4-1 (l)
9.9.96	Ecuador	(a)	0-1 (w)	20.7.97	Ecuador	(h)	1-0 (w)
10.11.96	Bolivia	(a)	2-2 (d)	20.8.97	Bolivia	(h)	3-0 (w)
15.12.96	Venezuela	(a)	0-2 (w)	10.9.97	Venezuela	(h)	1-0 (w)
12.2.97	Argentina	(h)	0-1 (l)	16.11.97	Argentina	(a)	1-1 (d)

The flair and character associated with the Colombian side is fully demonstrated by the temperamental Faustino Asprilla. The awkward looking hitman is another yet to exhibit his full array of capabilities in a World Cup final. In France, can Asprilla (if fully fit) show the world what we all know he can do? Accompanying Asprilla in the goalscoring labours will be Antony De Avila, Ivan Valenciano or Freddy Rincon.

Despite their obvious attacking qualities, Colombia's inconsistency in defence could be their undoing. Goalkeeper Oscar Cordoba's unstable performance in the last tournament emphasises this point: he may share goalkeeping duties with Argentina-based Farid Mondragon. Even though these frailties could hinder Colombia's chances, they can look to their attacking options to pull them through.

ABOVE LEFT: The Columbian team about to play against Argentina in February 1997.

BELOW: Faustino Asprilla playing against Argentina in Columbia's 2-1 win in February 1997.

PLAYERS TO WATCH FOR

Faustino Asprilla
Freddy Rincon

FIRST ROUND MATCHES

Date	Opponents	Venue
15.6	Romania	Lyon
22.6	Tunisia	Montpellier
26.6	England	Lens

CROATIA

The standard bearer of a national side appearing for the first time on the world stage is the cunning Davor Suker, probably the most gifted Croatian player of all time. His style of play carries a mesmeric quality, his guile, his ball control, his goalscoring dimensions set him apart from so many of his peers. He is not the only member of the Croatian squad to be furnished with such gifts. Striking counterpart Goran Vlaovic (who nearly had to quit the game with medical problems) is a tenacious goal scorer with a touch of added flair, and the forceful promptings of Lazio's Alen Boksic, who can produce telling moments of class, should not be forgotten. Suker, Vlaovic and Boksic will not be short of players able to deliver the supplies for them to feed on. Those include the creative trio of Robert Prosinecki (now back in his home country with Croatia Zagreb), midfield dynamo Zvonimir Boban and the polished skills of Aljosa Asanovic (Derby County).

World Cup History
First appearance in finals

EUROPE GROUP 1

TEAM	P	W	D	L	G	PTS
Denmark	8	5	2	1	14-6	17
Croatia	**8**	**4**	**3**	**1**	**17-12**	**15**
Greece	8	4	2	2	11-4	14
Bosnia	8	3	0	5	9-14	9
Slovenia	8	0	1	7	5-20	1

THE ROAD TO FRANCE

9.10.96	Bosnia	(a)	1-4 (w)	10.9.97	Denmark	(a)	3-1 (l)
10.11.97	Greece	(h)	1-1 (d)	11.10.97	Slovenia	(a)	1-3 (w)
29.3.97	Denmark	(h)	1-1 (d)				
2.4.97	Slovenia	(h)	3-3 (d)	**Play-offs**			
30.4.97	Greece	(a)	0-1 (w)	29.10.97	Ukraine	(h)	2-0 (w)
6.9.97	Bosnia	(h)	3-2 (w)	15.11.97	Ukraine	(a)	1-1 (d)

Croatia's defensive lynch pin is Everton-based centre back Slaven Bilic, an uncompromising and tough-tackling man-marker. Bilic's defensive counterparts are selected from the solid Igor Stimac and the formidable Nikola Jerkan. Croatia also rely upon the surging runs of the two full-backs: during Euro '96 the task fell to Mario Stanic (more recognised as a midfield player) and Robert Jarni, whose left foot can be both subtle and thunderous.

The fiery Croatian temperament is a trait that can cause disciplinary problems. Miroslav Blazevic, the man in charge of guiding the Croats, would like to see this passion utilised for more positive purposes. The Croatian team is sure to set the World Cup alight with its dazzling football, and the Croats will prove defiant opponents for anyone who has to face them.

ABOVE LEFT: The Croatian team prepares to play against England in 1996.

BELOW: Davor Suker playing against Germany in June 1996.

PLAYERS TO WATCH FOR

Davor Suker
Robert Jarni
Zvonimir Boban

FIRST ROUND MATCHES

Date	Opponents	Venue
14.6	Jamaica	Lens
21.6	Japan	Nantes
26.6	Argentina	Bordeaux

NIGERIA

Nigeria will be hoping to build on recent international form. In the last three years the Super Eagles, have succeeded on three fronts. In 1994 they triumphed in the African Nations Cup; they reached the last 16 at USA '94; more recently they won gold at Atlanta '96. As the surprise package at the Olympics they dismissed Brazil (a team which included Ronaldo) in a thrilling semi-final, before conquering Argentina in the final. Their success was masterminded by the gawky looking Nwankwo Kanu, who has recently returned to the game following a number of serious medical problems. Kanu possesses sublime skill and ball control, he was nurtured through the Ajax school of football and is now in Italy with Inter Milan. He is accompanied in the Nigerian front line by a host of varying attacking options. The direct approach would incorporate the bustling Daniel Amokachi, the robust style of Rasheed Yekini and the imposing figure of Kanu. Nigeria's attacking party can also turn to the pace of Monaco's Victor Ikpeba and the illusive Finidi George at Real Betis. With the exception of Yekini, the Nigeria squad consists of a fairly

World Cup History
Previous finals: 1994
Best performance: 2nd round 1994

AFRICA GROUP 1

TEAM	P	W	D	L	G	PTS
Nigeria	**6**	**4**	**1**	**1**	**10-4**	**13**
Guinea	6	4	0	2	10-5	12
Kenya	6	3	1	2	11-12	10
Burkina Faso	6	0	0	6	7-17	0

THE ROAD TO FRANCE

9.11.96	Burkina Faso	(h) 2-0 (w)	27.4.97	Burkina Faso	(a) 1-2 (w)
12.1.97	Kenya	(a) 1-1 (d)	7.6.97	Kenya	(h) 3-0 (w)
5.4.97	Guinea	(h) 2-1 (w)	17.8.97	Guinea	(a) 1-0 (l)

young band of players although, despite their youth, a number of the team were present in 1994: Oliseh, Adepoju, George, Okocha, Amunike and Amokachi are all in their early 20s. The Nigerian squad has slowly developed together, and has distinguished itself in African footballing circles. The main core of the squad earn their crust in a mixture of overseas leagues ranging from England, Spain and France to Italy, Holland and Turkey; all have thrived as individuals and gelled as an international unit.

The centre of defence is made up of colossal Uche Okechukwu and the youthful duo of Taribo West and Celestine Babyaro; the midfield consists of the energetic Sunday Oliseh and the masterful Jay Jay Okocha. Equated with the mass of attacking choices the central section of the side is pretty airtight.

ABOVE LEFT: Nigerian team playing against Kenya in the group game in January 1997.

BELOW: Daniel Amokachi playing against Brazil.

PLAYERS TO WATCH FOR

Sunday Oliseh
Celestine Babyaro
Nwankwo Kanu

FIRST ROUND MATCHES

Date	Opponents	Venue
13.6	Spain	Nantes
19.6	Bulgaria	Paris
24.6	Paraguay	Toulouse

AUSTRIA

Coach Herbert Prohaska is aiming to direct his Austrian side to new heights, following their failure to qualify for the World Cup in 1994. Prohaska took over in 1993, after his success with Rapid Vienna. He piloted Austria through a difficult qualifying group. They managed victory over Sweden (who finished third in USA '94) both home and away, and the only blip during qualification was an away defeat to the Scots.

Leading hitman Anton Polster, despite his age, has lost none of his goalscoring prowess. Now the captain of the national side, he will be aiming to lead by example with his compelling style of play. He is sure to be the pivotal point for anything positive Austria can produce. Supplying him will be the job of the talented Andreas Herzog, currently with Bayern Munich; Heimo Pfeifenberger will be the figure to support Herzog's efforts.

World Cup History
Previous finals: 1934, 1954, 1958, 1978, 1982, 1990
Best performance: 3rd place 1954

EUROPE GROUP 4

TEAM	P	W	D	L	G	PTS
Austria	**10**	**8**	**1**	**1**	**17-4**	**25**
Scotland	10	7	2	1	15-3	23
Sweden	10	7	0	3	16-9	21
Latvia	10	3	1	6	10-14	10
Estonia	10	1	1	8	4-16	4
Belarus	10	1	1	8	5-21	4

THE ROAD TO FRANCE

31.8.96	Scotland	(h)	0-0 (d)	8.6.97	Latvia	(a)	1-3 (w)
9.10.96	Sweden	(a)	0-1 (w)	20.8.97	Estonia	(a)	0-3 (w)
9.11.96	Latvia	(h)	2-1 (w)	6.9.97	Sweden	(h)	1-0 (w)
2.4.97	Scotland	(a)	2-0 (l)	10.9.97	Belarus	(a)	0-1 (w)
30.4.97	Estonia	(h)	2-0 (w)	11.10.97	Belarus	(h)	4-0 (w)

Austria's defence centres on the formidable force of Borussia Dortmund's Wolfgang Feiersinger. He will be accompanied by another veteran of Italia '90 — Anton Pfeffer, an able cog in the defensive machine. Added to this is the gifted Harald Cerny, capable of surging runs to support his midfield and forays into the opposing defence.

Behind the back line is the established goalkeeper, Michael Konsel, currently with AS Roma. As proved in qualification Austria can keep clean sheets — seven in total, with just four goals conceded. At the other end they managed a creditable 17 goals from their 10 games. The Austrian side may be able to repel their opponents, but finding the goals to win games may prove more difficult. If Austria can find goals they could advance further than in Italia '90, but if they fail to do so, they will be going home early.

ABOVE LEFT: The Austrian team that won 4-0 in the group qualifier against Belarus in October 1997.

BELOW: Harald Cerny playing against Belarus.

PLAYERS TO WATCH FOR

Anton Polster
Harald Cerny

FIRST ROUND MATCHES

Date	Opponents	Venue
11.6	Cameroon	Toulouse
17.6	Chile	Saint-Etienne
23.6	Italy	Saint-Denis

CHILE

Chile has always been classed as one of South America's lesser footballing powers, but have put this myth aside to qualify for their sixth World Cup.

Chile has a modest record in the World Cup, failing to qualify for the second phase on three occasions. It was as host nation in 1962, that Chile experienced their greatest achievements, third behind Brazil and Czechoslovakia.

Chile's course to France was steered by Uruguayan-born coach Nelson Acosta, who was installed just prior to Chile's campaign to reach the finals. As with most South American nations, the emphasis is on attack. The main

World Cup History
Previous finals: 1930, 1950, 1962, 1966, 1970, 1974, 1982
Best performance: 3rd 1962

SOUTH AMERICAN GROUP

TEAM	P	W	D	L	G	PTS
Argentina	16	8	6	2	23-13	30
Paraguay	16	9	2	5	21-14	29
Colombia	16	8	4	4	23-15	28
Chile	**16**	**7**	**4**	**5**	**32-18**	**25**
Peru	16	7	4	5	19-20	25
Ecuador	16	6	3	7	22-21	21
Uruguay	16	6	3	7	18-21	21
Bolivia	16	4	5	7	18-21	17
Venezuela	16	0	3	13	8-41	3

THE ROAD TO FRANCE

2.6.96	Venezuela	(a)	1-1 (d)	12.2.97	Bolivia	(a)	1-1 (d)
7.7.96	Ecuador	(h)	4-1 (w)	30.4.97	Venezuela	(h)	6-0 (w)
1.9.96	Colombia	(a)	4-1 (l)	8.6.97	Ecuador	(a)	1-1 (d)
9.10.96	Paraguay	(a)	2-1 (l)	5.7.97	Colombia	(h)	4-1 (w)
12.10.97	Peru	(h)	4-0 (w)	20.7.97	Paraguay	(h)	2-1 (w)
12.11.96	Uruguay	(h)	1-0 (w)	20.8.97	Uruguay	(a)	1-0 (l)
15.12.96	Argentina	(a)	1-1 (d)	10.9.97	Argentina	(h)	1-2 (l)
12.1.97	Peru	(a)	2-1 (l)	16.11.97	Bolivia	(h)	3-0 (w)

thrust is supplied by the powerful Ivan Zamorano (at Internazionale in Italy), whose direct type of football is complemented by the youthful goal scoring exuberance of Marcelo Salas currently with the giants of River Plate, and it would take a fee in excess of £12 million for him to be lured away.

The character given the duty of protecting any advantage Chile obtain will be goalkeeper Nelson Tapia. Forming a barrier in front of him will be the likely quartet of Reyes, Margas, Ponce and Christian Castanedas — a defence which kept only four clean sheets during qualification, and conceded 18 goals.

The Chilean side definitely has the class in Zamorano and Salas to threaten most teams, but may struggle against more educated defences. It could prove a long trip for the Chileans and may also prove to be a brief visit to France '98.

ABOVE LEFT: The Chilean team that lost 1-2 to Argentina in the group qualifier in October 1997.

BELOW: Esteban Valencia playing against Bolivia in November 1997.

PLAYERS TO WATCH FOR

Marcelo Salas
Ivan Zamorano

FIRST ROUND MATCHES

Date	Opponents	Venue
11.6	Italy	Bordeaux
17.6	Austria	Saint-Etienne
23.6	Cameroon	Nantes

BELGIUM

Vincenzo Scifo will be appearing in his fourth consecutive World Cup finals, and has been the nucleus for Belgium's conquests on the World Cup stage. Beside Scifo in the Belgian midfield are further established performers. Franky van der Elst has been an integral part of Belgium's past campaigns, but is probably beyond his best, although still has a tenacity and fighting spirit which has kept him in the Belgian squad. Another footballer from the same mould is Bruges' Lorenzo Staelens, a snappy tackler and determined ball winner. The creative aspects of the Belgian formation are centred around the irrepressible Scifo, the sprightly Danny Boffin and the goalscoring Marc Wilmots. These three will be looking to deliver a quality service for their front men. Boffin is a traditional winger, while Wilmots' strengths are his powerful running and his accurate long-range shooting.

Hoping to make the most of their teammates'

World Cup History
Previous finals: 1930, 1934, 1938, 1954, 1970, 1982, 1986, 1990, 1994
Best performance: 4th place 1986

EUROPE GROUP 7

TEAM	P	W	D	L	G	PTS
Holland	8	6	1	1	26-4	19
Belgium	**8**	**6**	**0**	**2**	**20-11**	**18**
Turkey	8	4	2	2	21-9	14
Wales	8	2	1	5	20-21	7
San Marino	8	0	0	8	0-42	0

THE ROAD TO FRANCE

31.8.96	Turkey	(h)	2-1 (w)	6.9.97	Holland	(a)	3-1 (l)
9.10.96	San Marino	(a)	0-3 (w)	11.10.97	Wales	(h)	3-2 (w)
14.12.96	Holland	(h)	0-3 (l)				
29.3.97	Wales	(a)	1-2 (w)	**Play-offs**			
30.4.97	Turkey	(a)	1-3 (w)	29.10.97	Rep Ireland	(a)	1-1 (d)
7.6.97	San Marino	(h)	6-0 (w)	15.11.97	Rep Ireland	(h)	2-1 (w)

promptings will be a selection of adept strikers. Brazilian-born Luis Oliveira can call upon his pace and awkward dribbling style; PSV Eindhoven's Luc Nilis is another player who possesses great technique and ability. Beside Nilis is 'the Beast': Gilles de Bilde, a tricky and evasive goalpoacher.

Directing will be coach George Leekens, who has established himself with the Belgian team, following his installation in early 1997. In previous tournaments Belgium have not experienced their fair share of good luck. In 1990 a last minute winner in extra time cost them a place in the quarter finals, while in 1994 they were refused a blatant penalty kick at the same stage. If they manage to earn their luck and can give their strikers a constant supply of goalscoring chances, they should advance to the second phase at the very least.

ABOVE LEFT: The Belgian team that lost to Holland in the group qualifier in December 1996.

BELOW: Luc Nilis playing for Belgium in the 3-0 defeat against Holland in December 1996.

PLAYERS TO WATCH FOR

Enzo Scifo
Luc Nilis
Luis Oliveira

FIRST ROUND MATCHES

Date	Opponents	Venue
13.6	Holland	Saint-Denis
20.6	Mexico	Bordeaux
25.6	South Korea	Paris

PARAGUAY

The director of Paraguay's progress in France will be coach Paolo Cesar Carpeggiani, a Brazilian who enjoyed domestic league success with Flamengo in his home country, as well as an international playing career. If you collate Carpeggiani's experience with Paraguay's qualification record, they may have a chance. Their run in to France saw them defeat the talented Colombians, fellow qualifiers Chile and France '98 dark horses Argentina.

An integral part of Paraguay's chances will be the flamboyant goalkeeper (and scorer) Jose Luis Chilavert. Seen by some experts as the most accomplished custodian in the world game, Chilavert — who keeps goal for Velez Sarsfield in Argentina — will influence his

World Cup History
Previous finals: 1930, 1950, 1958, 1986,
Best performance: 2nd round 1986

SOUTH AMERICAN GROUP

TEAM	P	W	D	L	G	PTS
Argentina	16	8	6	2	23-13	30
Paraguay	**16**	**9**	**2**	**5**	**21-14**	**29**
Colombia	16	8	4	4	23-15	28
Chile	16	7	4	5	32-18	25
Peru	16	7	4	5	19-20	25
Ecuador	16	6	3	7	22-21	21
Uruguay	16	6	3	7	18-21	21
Bolivia	16	4	5	7	18-21	17
Venezuela	16	0	3	13	8-41	3

THE ROAD TO FRANCE

24.4.96	Colombia	(a)	1-0 (l)	2.4.97	Colombia	(h)	2-1 (w)
2.6.96	Uruguay	(a)	0-2 (w)	30.4.97	Uruguay	(h)	3-1 (w)
1.9.96	Argentina	(a)	1-1 (d)	6.7.97	Argentina	(h)	1-2 (l)
9.10.96	Chile	(h)	2-1 (w)	20.7.97	Chile	(a)	2-1 (l)
10.11.96	Ecuador	(h)	1-0 (w)	20.8.97	Ecuador	(a)	2-1 (l)
15.12.96	Bolivia	(a)	0-0 (d)	10.9.97	Bolivia	(h)	2-1 (w)
12.1.97	Venezuela	(a)	0-2 (w)	12.10.97	Venezuela	(h)	1-0 (w)
12.2.97	Peru	(h)	2-1 (w)	16.11.97	Peru	(a)	1-0 (l)

teammates with his obvious qualities. Chilavert can often be found directing set-pieces around his opponents' area (and on occasion finding the net); he also frequently tries his hand at penalty kicks. More recognisable front runners are Aristides Rojas and the imposing figure of Jose Cardozo. Supplying opportunities for the strikers will be the young Julio Enciso, older performers Daniel Bourdier and Francisco Arce. The defensive aspects of Paraguay's structure may focus on the more experienced Catalino Rivarola, and younger defenders — Carlos Gamarra and the classy Celso Ayala.

If they can maintain discipline and cohesion, the Paraguayans could open a few eyes in France. As with all South American nations they have a vivid and fervent following, which will be hoping their boys can produce competent displays, and keep them in the tournament for longer than the group phase.

ABOVE LEFT: The Paraguay team that lost to Ecuador in Quito, August 1997.

BELOW: Francisco Javier playing against Chile in June 1997.

PLAYERS TO WATCH FOR
Jose Luis Chilavert

FIRST ROUND MATCHES

Date	Opponents	Venue
12.6	Bulgaria	Montpellier
19.6	Spain	Saint-Etienne
24.6	Nigeria	Toulouse

SAUDI ARABIA

In USA '94, Saudi Arabia surprised everyone: they will be hoping at least to reproduce those performances. In France they will be under the watchful eye of German coach Otto Pfister, who took up the reins in early 1997.

The Saudis became the 24th qualifier with somewhat uninspiring displays but it did demonstrate their determination to battle for victory. Lack of goal scoring could be a major difficulty, and a hindrance to Saudi Arabia's aspirations of creating further upsets.

With their shortage of goal scoring abilities, undoubtedly pressure could fall on their defensive areas. This could see goalkeeper Mohammed Al Deayea being kept extremely busy, but — as he showed in USA '94 — he has the necessary agility and courage to emerge as Saudi Arabia's star performer. The 'keeper's elasticity and reflexes may repel numerous attacks, but without solidity in front of him it would be no good. The current crop of Saudi players has produced a relatively young squad but, despite this, many of the party have over 80

World Cup History
Previous finals: 1994
Best performance: 1st round 1994

ASIA GROUP A

TEAM	P	W	D	L	G	PTS
Saudi Arabia	**8**	**4**	**2**	**2**	**8-6**	**14**
Iran	8	3	3	2	13-8	12
China	8	3	2	3	11-14	11
Qatar	8	3	1	4	7-10	10
Kuwait	8	2	2	4	7-8	8

THE ROAD TO FRANCE

14.9.97	Kuwait	(h)	2-1 (w)		17.10.97	Kuwait	(a)	2-1 (l)
19.9.97	Iran	(a)	1-1 (d)		24.10.97	Iran	(h)	1-0 (w)
3.10.97	China	(a)	1-0 (l)		6.11.97	China	(h)	1-1 (d)
11.10.97	Qatar	(h)	1-0 (w)		12.11.97	Qatar	(a)	0-1 (w)

international caps under their belts. One of these players is the influential Sami Al Jaber, who will be the pivotal point around which any attacking ideas revolve. Al Jaber will rely on his intelligence in creating and taking any opportunities that may arise.

Within the midfield department, Khamis Al Dossari will be Saudi Arabia's key component. If coach Pfister can obtain support for his two most gifted individuals, they may well raise a few eyebrows once more in France. Pfister will be aiming to use his expertise in procuring the most from his squad, as he managed with Ghana in leading them to the African Nations Final in 1992.

With their colourful and enthusiastic fans cheering on their heroes, the Saudis could cause headaches for opponents who underestimate their abilities; nevertheless Saudi Arabia's stay in the World Cup could be a short one.

ABOVE LEFT: Saudi Arabian team line up at Qatar.

BELOW: Fahad Mehalel playing in the 2-0 win against Qatar in November 1997.

PLAYERS TO WATCH FOR
Mohammed Al Deayea
Sami Al Jaber

FIRST ROUND MATCHES

Date	Opponents	Venue
12.6	Denmark	Lens
18.6	France	Saint-Denis
24.6	South Africa	Bordeaux

IRAN

Political problems have dampened Iran's progression to World Cup finals over recent previous tournaments. On top of this, Iran's progress to France was not the most direct. They initially finished as a runner-up to Saudi Arabia. This was followed by a play-off on neutral territory with Japan (they were beaten with a golden goal extra-time winner). But they had a third bite of the World Cup 'cherry', and eventually advanced to the finals after a dramatic two-leg tie against Oceania qualifiers Australia. The first leg of the tie was in Tehran, and women were banned from attending the match; however 3,000 or so stormed through the gates to take their place in the 70,000 strong crowd.

The game ended 1–1 with the impetus firmly in the hands of the Australians. The second leg was played in Melbourne. The Australians showed early promise and took a 2–0 lead. With Australia's qualification imminent, the

World Cup History
Previous finals: 1978
Best performance: 1st round

ASIA GROUP A

TEAM	P	W	D	L	G	PTS
Saudi Arabia	8	4	2	2	8-6	14
Iran	**8**	**3**	**3**	**2**	**13-8**	**12**
China	8	3	2	3	11-14	11
Qatar	8	3	1	4	7-10	10
Kuwait	8	2	2	4	7-8	8

THE ROAD TO FRANCE

13.9.97	China	(a) 2-4 (w)	7.11.97	Qatar	(a) 2-0 (l)
19.9.97	Saudi Arabia	(h) 1-1 (d)			
26.9.97	Kuwait	(a) 1-1 (d)	**Play-offs**		
3.10.97	Qatar	(h) 3-0 (w)	16.11.97	Japan	(a) 3-2 (l)
17.10.97	China	(h) 4-1 (w)	22.11.97	Australia	(h) 1-1 (d)
24.10.97	Saudi Arabia	(a) 1-0 (l)	29.11.97	Australia	(a) 2-2 (d)
31.10.97	Kuwait	(h) 0-0 (d)	(won on away goals)		

Iranian side started to fight back, pulling a goal back. In the dying moments they claimed a dramatic equaliser had reached the World Cup for the first time in 20 years, on the away goals ruling.

Prior to this ecstatic moment, Iran's major landmark had been their demolition of the hapless Maldive Islands 17–0. This record haul included seven goals from striker Karim Bakeri.

It would appear that goal machine Bakeri will be the man to watch when Iran take to the field in France. Leading the side in the finals will be Brazilian coach Valdier Viera, who despite behind the scenes disharmony, gelled his team into a united force.

The fanatical Iran fans will be hoping Viera can carry on his magic, and see their heroes cause some shocks during 1998. Despite the cohesion instilled to their side they are unlikely to advance beyond the preliminary group stages.

ABOVE LEFT: Iran just before playing Qatar, November 1997.

BELOW: Khodadad Azizi playing for Iran against Qatar in the group match of November 1997.

PLAYERS TO WATCH FOR
Karim Bakeri

FIRST ROUND MATCHES

Date	Opponents	Venue
14.6	Yugoslavia	Saint-Etienne
21.6	USA	Lyon
25.6	Germany	Montpellier

JAPAN

With the 2002 World Cup being hosted jointly by Japan and Korea, the Japanese will be looking to provide their public with a competent performance in France, to show that they will be worthy of being hosts. A catalyst for Japan finally reaching the World Cup stage could be the continued triumph of the J-League (Japan's national league). With the development of the league and the arrival of a number of top stars, the game in Japan has flourished. Home-grown talent has learnt and thrived alongside more accomplished names in the world game, including talents such as Zico, Dunga, Schillaci, Jorginho, Stoijkovic and Laudrup.

Japan's debut in the World Cup will be overseen by coach Takeshi Okada, appointed in autumn 1996. In Japanese football the emphasis is put on fast moving, attacking play, concentrating on passing and skill, rather than the more physical aspects of the game. Okada has continued in this vein.

The qualifying programme was intense, cul-

World Cup History
First appearance in finals

ASIA GROUP B

TEAM	P	W	D	L	G	PTS
South Korea	8	6	1	1	19-7	19
Japan	**8**	**3**	**4**	**1**	**17-9**	**13**
UAE	8	2	3	3	9-12	9
Uzbekistan	8	1	3	4	13-18	6
Kazakhstan	8	1	3	4	7-19	6

THE ROAD TO FRANCE

7.9.97	Uzbekistan	(h)	6-3 (w)	1.11.97	South Korea	(a)	0-2 (w)
19.9.97	UAE	(a)	0-0 (d)	8.11.97	Kazakhstan	(h)	5-1 (w)
28.9.97	South Korea	(h)	1-2 (l)				
4.10.97	Kazakstan	(a)	1-1 (d)	**Play-off**			
11.10.97	Uzbekistan	(a)	1-1 (d)	16.11.97	Iran	(h)	3-2 (w)
26.10.97	UAE	(h)	1-1 (d)				

minating in a play-off fixture with Iran on neutral territory. This contest went right to the wire, with Japan claiming their place in France with a golden goal winner in extra time.

The side will revolve around two players: captain Masima Ihara, an influential central defender with commanding leadership qualities, will play alongside fellow defenders Akita, Narahashi and Soma. The driving force behind their attacking efforts will be live-wire Kazu Miura (the first Japanese international to play in Italy's Serie A). Gifted with supreme ball control, he is set to be the standard bearer for any Japanese accomplishments.

The Japanese will certainly be an interesting team to watch, with their confident pacy passing game; they may, however, find it difficult to breach teams with more efficient defensive systems. Whatever happens Japan and their enthusiastic following will enjoy their time in France.

ABOVE LEFT: The Japan team that played in the Umbro Cup.

BELOW: Kazu Miura playing against England in the Umbro Cup.

PLAYERS TO WATCH FOR

Kazu Miura
Masima Ihara

FIRST ROUND MATCHES

Date	Opponents	Venue
14.6	Argentina	Toulouse
20.6	Croatia	Nantes
26.6	Jamaica	Lyon

SOUTH KOREA

France '98 hold special significance for the Koreans, as in 2002 they will be joint World Cup hosts with Japan. A stirring performance will increase support at home for when they welcome the world in four years time.

Governing the South Korean bid for success in France will be coach Bum Kun-Cha. His first goal will be to gain a first victory for South Korea at a World Cup finals, and to guide them beyond the group stages for the first time. Both of these ambitions may be above his squad's capabilities. Goals have proved a problem in previous competitions: South Korea have scored just seven times in their 11 competitive matches, as against the 33 put past them! The discipline instilled by Bum Kun-Cha may provide them with a more solid foundation both in attacking and defensive situations.

The authoritative figure of captain Hong Myung-Bo should provide the stability to influence others around him, and inspire them to greater efforts. Another feature of Hong Myung-Bo's armoury is the ferocity of his shooting.

World Cup History
Previous finals: 1954, 1986, 1990, 1994
Best performance: 1st round

ASIA GROUP B

TEAM	P	W	D	L	G	PTS
South Korea	8	6	1	1	19-7	19
Japan	8	3	4	1	17-9	13
UAE	8	2	3	3	9-12	9
Uzbekistan	8	1	3	4	13-18	6
Kazakhstan	8	1	3	4	7-19	6

THE ROAD TO FRANCE

6.9.97	Kazakstan	(h)	3-0 (w)	11.10.97	Kazakstan	(a)	1-1 (d)
12.9.97	Uzbekistan	(h)	2-1 (w)	18.10.97	Uzbekistan	(a)	1-5 (w)
28.9.97	Japan	(a)	1-2 (w)	1.11 97	Japan	(h)	0-2 (l)
4.10.97	UAE	(h)	3-0 (w)	9.11.97	UAE	(a)	1-3 (w)

South Korea will rely heavily on his prowess in both defence and more prominent forward areas. Beside Hong Myung-Bo will be further experience in the shape of the educated Seok-Ju Ha (who has over 70 caps), hoping to assist in the protection of the South Korean goal. The defence will no doubt be stretched during their early encounters, but if they can repel all that is thrown at them they may reproduce the performances shown in 1994: following draws with Bolivia and Spain (after being two goals down), they almost reached the second phase with a battling show against Germany. Trailing by three goals at the break, South Korea claimed two of their own, but failed to conjure the third, that their second half courage deserved. This fighting spirit will again be evident in France, but they will require more than grit and determination if they are to avoid a first round exit.

ABOVE LEFT: The South Korean team that beat the UAE in November 1997.

BELOW: Do-Hoon Kim playing in the 3-1 win against the UAE.

PLAYERS TO WATCH FOR

Hong Myung-Bo
Seok-Ju Ha

FIRST ROUND MATCHES

Date	Opponents	Venue
13.6	Mexico	Lyon
20.6	Holland	Marseille
25.6	Belgium	Paris

YUGOSLAVIA

The problems in the Balkans mean that this is the first tournament for the team since returning to international competitions. Their last exploits saw them reach the quarter finals of the World Cup in Italia '90.

A shining prospect in 1990 was the brilliant Dragan Stoijkovic, currently playing in Japan's J-League. The cunning Yugoslav still possesses the talents which led him to the glamour of Italy's Serie A. Aiding the craft of Stoijkovic will be the Lazio-based Vladimir Jugovic; he will partner his captain in supplying ammunition for Yugoslavia's front men. Further expressive play will revolve around teammates Branko Brnovic and Slavisa Jokanovic, who complete a competent midfield quartet. Through this tireless endeavour and craft, Stoijkovic, Brnovic, Jugovic and Jokanovic will be aiming to provide

World Cup History
Previous finals: 1930, 1950, 1954, 1958, 1962, 1974, 1982, 1990
Best performance: 4th 1930, 1962

EUROPE GROUP 6

TEAM	P	W	D	L	G	PTS
Spain	10	8	2	0	26-6	26
Yugoslavia	**10**	**7**	**2**	**1**	**29-7**	**23**
Czech Rep	10	5	1	4	16-6	16
Slovakia	10	5	1	4	18-14	16
Faroe Islands	10	2	0	8	10-31	6
Malta	10	0	0	10	2-37	0

THE ROAD TO FRANCE

24.4.96	Faroe Is	(h)	3-1 (w)	8.6.97	Slovakia	(h)	2-0 (w)
2.6.96	Malta	(h)	6-0 (w)	10.9.97	Slovakia	(a)	1-1 (d)
6.10.96	Faroe Is	(a)	1-8 (w)	11.10.97	Malta	(a)	0-5 (w)
10.11.96	Czech Rep	(h)	1-0 (w)				
14.12.96	Spain	(a)	2-0 (l)	**Play-offs**			
2.4.97	Czech Rep	(a)	1-2 (w)	29.10.97	Hungary	(a)	1-7 (w)
30.4.97	Spain	(h)	1-1 (d)	15.11.97	Hungary	(h)	5-1 (w)

goalscoring opportunities for their even more awesome strike force. The forward line comprises the flamboyant pair of Pedrag Mijatovic and Dejan Savicevic.

Coach Slobodan Santrac (who took charge in 1994) will be hoping to motivate his troops to the sort of expressive performances they showed in 1990. Goalscoring will prove little obstacle: the team found the net 29 times during the group stage of qualification, while only conceding seven.

This imposing form will make Yugoslavia a match for any of the other nations in France, including the more established footballing countries such as Brazil, Germany and France. Yugoslavia could prove a real revelation during the summer of '98.

ABOVE LEFT: The Yugoslavian team against Spain in December 1996.

BELOW: Savo Milosevic playing against Hungary in the 7-1 win in the play-offs in October 1996.

PLAYERS TO WATCH FOR

Pedrag Mijatovic
Sinsia Mihajlovic
Dejan Savicevic

FIRST ROUND MATCHES

Date	Opponents	Venue
14.6	Iran	Saint-Etienne
21.6	Germany	Lens
25.6	USA	Nantes

FRANCE 98 FIXTURES

GROUP A
Wed June 10
Brazil v Scotland, Saint-Denis *4.30pm*
Morocco v Norway, Montpellier *8pm*

Tue June 16
Scotland v Norway, Bordeaux *4.30pm*
Brazil v Morocco, Nantes *8pm*

Tue June 23
Brazil v Norway, Marseille *8pm*
Scotland v Morocco, Saint-Etienne *8pm*

GROUP B
Thu June 11
Italy v Chile, Bordeaux *4.30pm*
Cameroon v Austria, Toulouse *8pm*

Wed June 17
Chile v Austria, Saint-Etienne *4.30pm*
Italy v Cameroon, Montpellier *8pm*

Tue June 23
Italy v Austria, Saint-Denis *3pm*
Chile v Cameroon, Nantes *3pm*

GROUP C
Fri June 12
Saudi Arabia v Denmark, Lens *4.30pm*
France v South Africa, Marseille *8pm*

Thu June 18
South Africa v Denmark, Toulouse *4.30pm*
France v Saudi Arabia, Saint-Denis *8pm*

Wed June 24
France v Denmark, Lyon *3pm*
South Africa v Saudi Arabia, Bordeaux *3pm*

GROUP D
Fri June 12
Paraguay v Bulgaria, Montpellier *1.30pm*

Sat June 13
Spain v Nigeria, Nantes *1.30pm*

Fri June 19
Nigeria v Bulgaria, Paris *4.30pm*
Spain v Paraguay, Saint-Etienne *8pm*

Wed June 24
Spain v Bulgaria, Lens *8pm*
Nigeria v Paraguay, Toulouse *8pm*

GROUP E
Sat June 13
South Korea v Mexico, Lyon *4.30pm*
Holland v Belgium, Saint-Denis *8pm*

Sat June 20
Belgium v Mexico, Bordeaux *1.30pm*
Holland v South Korea, Marseille *8pm*

Thu June 25
Holland v Mexico, Saint-Etienne *3pm*
Belgium v South Korea, Paris *3pm*

GROUP F
Sun June 14
Yugoslavia v Iran, Saint-Etienne *1.30pm*

Mon June 15
Germany v United States, Paris *8pm*

Sun June 21
Germany v Yugoslavia, Lens *4.30pm*
United States v Iran, Lyons *8pm*

Thu June 25
Germany v Iran, Montpellier *8pm*
United States v Yugoslavia, Nantes *8pm*

GROUP G
Mon June 15
England v Tunisia, Marseille *1.30pm*
Romania v Colombia, Lyon *4.30pm*

Mon June 22
Colombia v Tunisia, Montpellier *4.30pm*
Romania v England, Toulouse *8pm*

Fri June 26
Romania v Tunisia, Saint-Denis *8pm*
Colombia v England, Lens *8pm*

GROUP H
Sun June 14
Argentina v Japan, Toulouse *4.30pm*
Jamaica v Croatia, Lens 8pm

Sat June 20
Japan v Croatia, Nantes *4.30pm*

Sun June 21
Argentina v Jamaica, Paris *1.30pm*

Fri June 26
Argentina v Croatia, Bordeaux *3pm*
Japan v Jamaica, Lyon *3pm*

FRANCE 98 FIXTURES

SECOND ROUND

Sat June 27

| **Match 1** 8pm | Winner Group **A** v Runner-up Group **B** | Paris |
| **Match 2** 3.30pm | Winner Group **B** v Runner-up Group **A** | Marseille |

Sun June 28

| **Match 3** 3.30pm | Winner Group **C** v Runner-up Group **D** | Lens |
| **Match 4** 8pm | Winner Group **D** v Runner-up Group **C** | Saint-Denis |

QUARTER – FINALS

Fri July 3

| **Match A** 8pm | Winner Match **1** v Winner Match **4** | Nantes |
| **Match B** 3.30pm | Winner Match **2** v Winner Match **3** | Saint-Denis |

BELOW: Jurgen Kohler celebrates winning the World Cup, Italia '90.

MON JUNE 29

Match 5 8pm   Winner Group **E** v Runner-up Group **F**   Toulouse

Match 6 3.30pm   Winner Group **F** v Runner-up Group **E**   Montpellier

TUE JUNE 30

Match 7 3.30pm   Winner Group **G** v Runner-up Group **H**   Bordeaux

Match 8 8pm   Winner Group **H** v Runner-up Group **G**   Saint-Etienne

---

SAT JULY 4

Match C 3.30pm   Winner Match **5** v Winner Match **8**   Marseille

Match D 8pm   Winner Match **6** v Winner Match **7**   Lyon

SEMI – FINALS

Tue July 7 8pm   Winner Match **A** v Winner Match **C**   Nantes

Wed July 8 3.30pm   Winner Match **B** v Winner Match **D**   Saint-Denis

---

THIRD AND FOURTH PLACE

Sat July 11 8pm   PARIS

FINAL

Sun July 12 8pm   SAINT-DENIS

NOTES